VANITY FAIR

A Novel without a Hero

TWAYNE'S MASTERWORK STUDIES

Robert Lecker, Editor

VANITY FAIR

A Novel without a Hero

Edgar F. Harden

TWAYNE PUBLISHERS
An Imprint of Simon & Schuster Macmillan
New York

Prentice Hall International
London Mexico City New Delhi Singapore Sydney Toronto

Twayne's Masterwork Series No. 157

Vanity Fair: A Novel without a Hero
Edgar F. Harden

Twayne Publishers
An Imprint of Simon & Schuster Macmillan
866 Third Avenue
New York, New York 10022

Library of Congress Cataloging-in-Publication Data

Harden, Edgar F.
    Vanity Fair : a novel without a hero / Edgar F. Harden.
        p.   cm.—(Twayne's masterworks series : no. 157)
    Includes bibliographical references and index.
    ISBN 0-8057-8390-3 (alk. paper).—ISBN 0-8057-4460-6 (pbk. alk. paper)
    1. Thackeray, William Makepeace, 1811–1863. Vanity Fair.   I. Title.   II.
Series: Twayne's masterwork studies : no 157.
PR5618.H37   1995
823'.8—dc20   95-6208
                                                                                           CIP

The paper used in this publication meets the minimum requirements of American National Standard for Information Sciences—Permanence of Paper for Printed Library Materials. ANSI Z3948–1984. ∞ ™

10 9 8 7 6 5 4 3 2 1 (hc)
10 9 8 7 6 5 4 3 2 1 (pb)

Printed in the United States of America

For my son Edgar

"The great sin . . . is to assume that something that has been read once has been read forever. As a[n] . . . example I mention Thackeray's *Vanity Fair*. People are expected to read it during their university years. But you are mistaken if you think you read Thackeray's book then; you read a lesser book of your own. It should be read again when you are 36, which is the age of Thackeray when he wrote it. It should be read for a third time when you are 56, 66, 76, in order to see how Thackeray's irony stands up to your own experience of life. . . . [Y]ou really should take another look at a great book, in order to find out how great it is, or how great it has remained to you. . . . *Nobody ever reads the same book twice.*"

Robertson Davies, "The Tanner Lectures on Human Values"

Contents

Note on the References

All quotations from *Vanity Fair* come from the standard critical edition by Peter L. Shillingsburg (New York and London: Garland Publishing, 1989), but citations are to chapter numbers so that readers can easily refer to whatever edition of the novel they happen to be using.

Nos. XIX. & XX.]   JULY.   [Price 2s.

Vanity Fair:

PEN AND PENCIL SKETCHES OF ENGLISH SOCIETY.

BY W. M. THACKERAY,

Author of " The Irish Sketch Book ;" " Journey from Cornhill to Grand Cairo ;" of " Jeames's Diary"
and the " Snob Papers " in " Punch ;" &c. &c.

LONDON:
PUBLISHED AT THE PUNCH OFFICE, 85, FLEET STREET.
J. MENZIES, EDINBURGH ; J. M'LEOD, GLASGOW ; J. M'GLASHAN, DUBLIN.

1848.

[Bradbury & Evans, Printers, Whitefriars.]

Chronology:

William Makepeace Thackeray's Life and Works

1811	William Makepeace Thackeray born in Calcutta to Richmond Thackeray, a prosperous official of the British East India Company, and Anne Becher.
1814	Napoleon abdicates; exiled to Elba.
1815	Napoleon returns to power; defeated at Waterloo; exiled to St. Helena. Thackeray's father dies, leaving a large estate.
1817	Thackeray comes to England, stopping at St. Helena. His mother, still in India, marries Captain Henry Carmichael-Smyth.
1817–21	Attends school in Southampton, then in Chiswick, near London.
1820	George IV becomes king. Thackeray's mother comes to England with her husband.
1822–28	Attends Charterhouse School in London.

Chronology

1829–30	Attends Trinity College, Cambridge; leaves without a degree.
1830	William IV becomes king.
1830–31	Lives in Weimar, Germany.
1831–33	Lives in London as law student and journalist.
1832	First Reform Bill passes, abolishing "rotten" boroughs and increasing the numbers of those eligible to vote.
1833	Loses most of his inheritance in the failure of an Indian bank.
1833–37	Lives in Paris as art student and journalist.
1836	*Flore et Zéphyr*, a collection of eight lithographs, published under the pseudonym *Theophile Wagstaffe*. Marries Isabella Shawe, member of an Anglo-Irish family.
1837	Settles in London, writing reviews, articles, and short comic fiction for magazines anonymously and under pseudonyms. Daughter Anne born. Victoria becomes queen.
1837–38	*The Yellowplush Papers* published serially with authorial illustrations in *Fraser's Magazine* under the pseudonym *Charles James Yellowplush* (additional paper in 1840).
1839–40	*Catherine* published serially with authorial illustrations in *Fraser's Magazine* under the pseudonym *Ikey Solomons*.
1840	Daughter Harriet born. *The Paris Sketch Book,* a collection of earlier magazine pieces and new work, published with authorial illustrations in two volumes under the pseudonym *M. A. Titmarsh*. Wife becomes insane.
1841	*Comic Tales and Sketches,* a collection of earlier magazine pieces, published with authorial illustrations in two volumes under the pseudonym, *Michael Angelo Titmarsh*.
1842	Travels to Ireland.
1843	*The Irish Sketch Book* published with authorial illustrations under the pseudonym *M. A. Titmarsh*, with dedication signed *W. M. Thackeray*.
1844	*Barry Lyndon* published serially in *Fraser's Magazine* under the pseudonym *Fitz-Boodle*.
1844–45	Travels to the Near East.
1846	*Notes of a Journey from Cornhill to Grand Cairo* published under the pseudonym *M. A. Titmarsh,* with dedication signed *W. M. Thackeray*.
1846–47	*The Book of Snobs* published serially with authorial illustrations in *Punch* under the rubric *By One of Themselves*.

Chronology

HISTORICAL AND LITERARY CONTEXT

1

Historical Context

Thackeray was born during 1811 in an age of revolutionary turmoil. Internationally, the dominant figure of the age was Napoleon, whose armies controlled much of Europe and with whom Great Britain was at war until his decisive defeat at Waterloo in 1815. Domestically, the most prominent figure was George, prince regent from 1811 to 1820 and king from 1820 to 1830, whose self-indulgent dandyism was a model for emulation and whose period of social dominance is the temporal setting for *Vanity Fair*. By the time Victoria became queen in 1837, Thackeray was essentially "formed": he had been educated, had been something of a Regency dandy, had traveled and lived abroad in Germany and in Paris as an art student, had seen most of his inheritance disappear, had begun to do newspaper work to support himself, had married, had become a father, and had just settled in London to supplement his newspaper work by writing articles and short comic fiction for magazines.

A young writer named Charles Dickens had just achieved outstanding success with a new form of publication. Already the author of a series of magazine pieces gathered in a single volume as *Sketches by Boz* (1836), Dickens had begun on 31 March 1836 to publish another series called *The Posthumous Papers of the Pickwick Club,* which grew into a novel (1836–37) appearing in a sequence of separate monthly parts with 32 pages of text, two full-page illustrations, several pages of advertisements, and green paper covers with an illustrated title page—selling for 1 shilling. It came to attract such an increased readership that Dickens, after beginning another novel, *Oliver Twist,* in issues (1837–38) of a monthly magazine of which he was editor, went on to publish a further novel in separate monthly parts, *Nicholas Nickleby* (1838–39). In short, Dickens and his publishers, Chapman and Hall, had established a significant new form for the novel—one that was not only published in separate monthly installments but also written month by month. It soon came to be used not only by Dickens in *Martin Chuzzlewit* (1843–44) and *Dombey and Son* (1846–48), but also by other novelists like Charles Lever in *Tom Burke of "Ours"* (1842–44), and by Thackeray in *Vanity Fair* (1847–48).

Thackeray's development as a writer of fiction, like that of Dickens, began in miscellaneous journalism—which at that time was typically written either anonymously or pseudonymously, thereby inviting the creation of a dramatized voice. In a magazine review of a book of etiquette whose author naïvely admired and wished to emulate fashionable life, Thackeray mockingly wrote his article in the language of a semiliterate footman. Seeing the possibilities of this persona, he then developed the footman into the narrator of a series of fictional sketches and gradually longer tales. Soon Thackeray was also creating many other personas: an extravagantly adventurous Irish major, a painter and art critic, a French soldier, the son of a purveyor of stolen goods, a barber, a clerk, an idle younger son of a baronet, an Irish rascal. Even as a writer of essays and books on travel, Thackeray habitually used pseudonyms. *Vanity Fair* was the first novel to print his own name on the title page.

As the identities of these various personas may suggest, Thackeray had not only a rich creativity but also one that wished to immerse itself in the realities of everyday life. The many escapist novels of his day activated his satirical and parodic energies, whether the novelistic escape was into fashionable life, romantic adventure, or sentimental melodrama. Indeed, his first novel, *Catherine* (1839–40), was a parody written in protest against the sentimentalizing of criminals and the grotesque distortions of thought and language that accompany such sentimentalizing. He had affinities with the great English realists of the previous century, Fielding in the novel and Hogarth in art, more than with the prominent novelists of the 1830s and early 1840s, most of whom are now forgotten: Ainsworth, Bulwer, Mrs. Gore, G. P. R. James, Lever, and others. Even the novels of Dickens, which he partly admired, seemed to him too fantastical and romantic. As he developed into the novelist who was to write *Vanity Fair*, his fiction grew more thickly populated and more dense with the palpable details of closely observed life, but he retained from his reading and his study of art the awareness of how a relatively few archetypal patterns underlie the multiplicities of daily experience.

Indeed, the title of his greatest novel emphasizes that awareness, coming as it does from a visionary masterpiece that for more than 150 years was read almost as much as the Bible and in all social classes: John Bunyan's *The Pilgrim's Progress from this World to That which is to come* (1678). One of the most formidable temptations through which Bunyan's Pilgrim has to pass is a fair called *Vanity Fair,* which lasts all the year and in which everything is for sale: countries, people, and aspirations, as well as things. In short, Vanity Fair is the world—*vanity* meaning precisely what the Preacher in the Bible's Book of Ecclesiastes meant by the term: that which is worthless because it exists only in time, "under the sun." In Thackeray's adaptation of the metaphor, we all spend our entire lives wandering giddily and frustratedly through Vanity Fair: its lures are irresistible and our desires unsatisfiable.

With *Vanity Fair,* Thackeray achieved his first major novelistic success, the culmination of 10 years of miscellaneous work. As well as a culmination, however, it was also a portent, for, as various critics have observed, *Vanity Fair* could have been the title of all his subsequent fiction. The title had come to him in a sudden flash of awareness during late 1846, and with it had come the epitomising metaphor for his understanding of human beings living in the world. His next three novels, although quite individual in nature, were especially effective in dramatizing this Thackerayan perspective: *Pendennis* (1848–50), *Henry Esmond* (1852), and *The Newcomes* (1853–55), helping to prompt George Eliot in 1857 to call him "the most powerful of living novelists."[1]

2

The Importance of the Work

1847 marks the beginning of an era in which the first masterpieces of English fiction since Jane Austen's *Emma* (1815) came to appear. *Vanity Fair* initiated this great procession, beginning with its first serial number for January, to be followed by *Jane Eyre* (1847), *Wuthering Heights* (1848), *Pendennis* (1848–50), *David Copperfield* (1849–50), *Henry Esmond* (1852), *Bleak House* (1852–53), *The Newcomes* (1853–55), *Adam Bede* (1859), and many others subsequently that completed the emergence of the novel as the dominant literary form during the last half of the nineteeth century. If *Vanity Fair* was the first great novel in this sequence, however, it was also Thackeray's first masterpiece and, by the time of its serial conclusion and immediately ensuing appearance in one-volume form during mid-1848, it had established his reputation as the one contemporary novelist whose genius rivaled that of Dickens.

As *Vanity Fair* began to appear, it struck its readers as being unlike any other work of contemporary fiction. For one thing, its scope of rendered human experience indicated that its subject was not the life of a single individual, or the lives of a small group of people living in a remote setting; rather, its subject seemed to be society itself:

a vastly complex interweaving of human relationships, mainly English, but including Belgian, French, and German, and mainly urban, though including countryfolk as well. The novel's vast scope extends from the extravagant opulence of George IV to the poverty of a ragged, young London crossing-sweeper, and includes among its social ranks nobles, titled gentry, diplomats, parliamentarians, soldiers, clergymen, civil officials, successful and unsuccessful middle-class merchants, governesses, female companions, schoolmasters and schoolmistresses, students, gamekeepers, clerks, maids, butlers, charwomen, grooms, Continental "raffs," and a host of other characters.

Along with this broad diversity of human life comes a rich multiplicity of clearly observed objects that give specific, concrete definition to the lives lived among them and to the values of the people who lead those lives. All this literal and emblematic detail is mediated to us, moreover, by a very cosmopolitan narrator who also understands all the ways in which human beings communicate their true nature, no matter how much they try to conceal it. Having lived *in* the world, he knows how it operates, and he deeply understands how to evaluate human conduct. Especially, of course, he shows us how all the characters are trapped in their social roles, whether they passively accept them, or whether they futilely try to adopt the social roles of others. He shows us how *patterned* our human behavior is, and how our seemingly individual motives and actions repeatedly reveal themselves to be analogues of the motives and actions of other people.

Thackeray's novel is also distinctive for its prevailingly ironic tone, irony being the perfect mode for perceiving, evaluating, and articulating the discrepancy not only between the pretentions and the actualities of human motives, but also between the moral promptings of human beings (if they have any left) and their conduct. Here again we see the narrator's great range and sophistication, as his ironic mode extends from cool, pointed, devastating satire, to lighthearted, playful mockery that engages us with its humor. We can be grateful for Thackeray's individualistic recreation of Vanity Fair, for unlike Bunyan he has a marvelous comic sense.

In short, the richness of *Vanity Fair* appears in many ways: in the reverberance of its central metaphor, in the elaborateness and scope of its coherence, in the vitality and multiplicity of its characterization, in the ease and suppleness of its style, in the trenchancy and brilliance of its wit. Most fundamentally, it justifies our admiration because of its humanly scaled subversive challenge to our values and pretensions. That is why we should treasure it: because it accepts our human nature even while it reveals the glibness of our assumptions—about ourselves, our "society," and our ultimate destiny—as well as the deranged language and the destructive behavior that follow from those assumptions. It creates for us an unavoidable mirror.

3

Critical Reception

Critical judgment upon *Vanity Fair* began to appear in a series of magazine reviews starting in May 1847, not long after the beginning of its serial run, with a friendly but necessarily tentative notice of what Thackeray later called a novel "struggling to get a place in the world."[2] Then in June 1847 after the appearance of but six numbers came a forceful statement of recognition: "If Mr. Thackeray were by some unforseen accident to die to-morrow his name would be transmitted down to posterity . . . by his *Vanity Fair*."[3] The assessment, though with some challenge over the years, survives to this very day: in writing this novel he created his masterpiece.

The judgment of its distinctive superiority over his earlier creations was repeated in January 1848, but another reviewer had already expressed a dividedness that would often be voiced in the criticism published by Thackeray's Victorian contemporaries: admiration for the novelist's powerful presentation of his characters, especially Becky Sharp, and unhappiness with what the critic felt was Thackeray's preference "for the unpleasing."[4] Here we meet the central phenomenon governing the Victorian reception of Thackeray's novel: a conflict between the assumptions about human nature and conduct that motivate Thackeray's satirical purpose on the one hand, and the assumptions that govern his critics' expectations of what a novelist's performance ought to be on the other.

Thackeray's assumptions, like Bunyan's, challenge conventional optimistic beliefs that human beings are fundamentally virtuous. His intentions for his novel appear in several letters written during its period of composition and immediately thereafter. Writing to his mother in July 1847 following the publication of number 7 (chs. 23–25), he commented:

> Dont you see how odious all the people are in the book (with the exception of Dobbin)—behind whom all there lies a dark moral I hope. What I want is to make a set of people . . . greedy pompous mean perfectly self-satisfied for the most part and at ease about their superior virtue. Dobbin & poor Briggs are the only 2 people with real humility as yet. Amelia's is to come, when her scoundrel of a husband is well dead . . . ; when she has had sufferings, a child, and a religion—But she has at present a quality above most people . . . : LOVE—by wh. she shall be saved.[5]

Writing to a critic in March 1848 who had termed *Vanity Fair* Thackeray's greatest work, but had complained that in it the "people are all scamps, scoundrels, or humbugs,"[6] Thackeray replied, "I am quite aware of the dismal roguery wh. goes all through the Vanity Fair story—and God forbid that the world should be like it altogether: though I fear it is more like it than we like to own. But my object is to make every body engaged . . . in the pursuit of Vanity and I must carry my story through."[7] In effect, he was pointing out implications of the novel's running head at the top of every other page, which later appeared as a revised subtitle, "A Novel without a Hero," but Thackeray might also have observed, as one critic did, that he was likewise careful not to raise villainy to too high a pitch: in the characters of *Vanity Fair* we are meant to recognize ourselves, our friends, and our acquaintances.[8]

In September 1848 after a generally favorable critical reviewer had nevertheless also objected to what he saw as the novel's almost unrelieved depiction of "egotism, faithlessness, and low depravities,"[9] Thackeray responded: "my object . . . is to indicate, in cheerful terms, that we are for the most part an abominably foolish and selfish people 'desperately wicked' and all eager after vanities. Everybody is you see in that book,—for instance if I had made Amelia a higher order of woman there would have been no vanity in Dobbins falling in love with her." He went on to indicate an ethical, indeed religious, purpose: "I want to leave everybody dissatisfied and unhappy at the end of the story—we ought all to be with our own and all other stories. Good God dont I see (in that maybe cracked and warped looking glass in which I am always looking) my own weaknesses wickednesses lusts follies shortcomings? . . . We must lift up our voices about these and howl to a congregation of fools: so much at least has been my endeavour."[10]

In short, Thackeray's acute sense of human folly motivates him to articulate his "dark moral," and to do so with determined consistency, though also with prevailing wit and humor. One critic termed him "the Fielding of the nineteenth century,"[11] and another agreed with this characterization because of Thackeray's ability to reveal hidden motives and to do so with cool irony. A number of the novel's reviewers, however, were disconcerted, objecting that Thackeray's "scepticism is pushed too far,"[12] that he insists on moving "too much in the direction of satire,"[13] and that "a cynical, sarcastic tone . . . too much pervades the work."[14] Even though reviewers generally found much to praise, they tended to share the view that *Vanity Fair* was "one of the most amusing, but also one of the most distressing books we have read."[15] One critic succinctly identified the basis for disagreement by saying that Thackeray's "philosophy [is] tainted"[16]—a philosophy that a number of critics wanted him to moderate.

Thackeray's critics also addressed the issues of artistic coherence and style. Several of them were concerned that composing and publishing a novel serially prevented a writer from thoroughly conceiving the whole work in advance and organizing "a well-constructed story."[17] For all their emphasis upon lively characterization, which they shared with many nineteenth-century readers, they also wanted a rather highly articulated plot. Other reviewers, however, praised *Vanity Fair*'s freedom from the Aristotelian formalities of a beginning, middle, and end, and they responded favorably to what they characterized as a narrative "flow"[18] that emulated "the progress of one's own life."[19]

Part of *Vanity Fair*'s originality in the eyes of such critics, therefore, was its freedom from contrivance—a quality that led one of them to call it "simply a history,"[20] by which she meant a sequence of everyday emotions and events unfolding in a natural progression. Analogously, Thackeray was praised for his fluency of style, critic after critic using the terms *easy* and *quiet* as they spoke of his "incomparably easy and unforced style,"[21] "so singularly winning, so easy, . . . felicitous, humourous and pleasant. . . . Trusting to truth and humour, he is the quietest perhaps of all contemporary writers."[22] By *quiet,* they meant both free from vehement opinions or "dogmatism,"[23] and free from stylistic "mannerism or affectation."[24] Several also commented on the uniqueness of a novel whose text was accompanied and enhanced by the writer's own illustrations, which exhibited powers "akin to the literary abilities of the author."[25]

A critic writing in July 1848, who termed the novel "one of the most original works of real genius that has of late been given to the world," felt that the uniqueness of the authorial perspective "impeded its first success."[26] In fact, *Vanity Fair* was at first only a very limited commercial success, but by the end of 1848 had sold roughly 7,500 copies per serial number.[27] If we assume some degree of multiple readership, we may estimate his audience as at least 10,000. Thackeray himself commented on the initially slow sales, but he also said that it "appears really immensely to increase my reputation."[28]

Critics of *Vanity Fair* in Thackeray's day were struck, then, by his unconventional assumptions about human nature and conduct, by his consistency in giving them fictional embodiment, and by his disconcerting blend of humorous with ironic presentation. Because these critics did not tend to think in formalistic terms, they customarily identified a novel's narrator with its author. Few of them, therefore, wrote about Thackeray's most unconventional authorial strategy in *Vanity Fair:* the creation of a narrator who intermittently not only addressed his audiences directly but also commented upon his own narrative. One critic who did remark upon these passages of commentary, however, emphasized their necessity: "there is nothing which could so little be spared."[29]

These qualities continued to be recognized in the second half of the nineteeth century, and critical evaluations continued to be based upon answers to questions like the following: Is Thackeray's humor genial or cynical? Are his truths wholesome or cruel? Does his satire support or undermine one's sense of reality? An individual writing in 1897 observed that estimation of Thackeray's writings seemed to depend chiefly upon whether a critic found a suitable "philosophy" in them. So too as the popularity of the serial novel declined and as tastes came to favor fiction that was more tightly organized, especially in keeping with principles of the scenic method derived from the theater, critics increasingly wanted a novel's narrator to be effaced from view, and they objected to a narrator's intervention into the narrative—though such objections, of course, deny a fundamental premise of Thackeray's novel.

Even a powerful advocate of the scenic method like Percy Lubbock in 1921, however, recognized the merits of its opposite: the panoramic method of *Vanity Fair*, which he described as the free wandering of Thackeray's imagination backward and forward over a broad social expanse swarming with people, as he presents his narrative "in a continuous flow of leisurely, contemplative reminiscence. . . . And that is the right way for the kind of story that Thackeray means to create. . . . The book is not the story of any of them, it is the story which they unite to tell."[30] For Lubbock, Thackeray's "masterly perspective" is that of "a long retrospective vision" articulated in "the general form of a discursive soliloquy, in which he gradually gathers up the long train of experience that he has in mind."[31]

The great body of modern Thackeray criticism appeared following World War II, initiated in part by the four volumes of largely unpublished letters made available in the four-volume edition of Gordon N. Ray, and by Ray's masterly two-volume biography, *Thackeray: The Uses of Adversity* (1955) and *Thackeray: The Age of Wisdom* (1958). This body of criticism has analyzed countless aspects of *Vanity Fair*, doing so in ways that range from traditional studies rooted in biography and literary history, to studies influenced by the

New Criticism, by psychology, and by other -ologies. Studies of literary relationships have included discussion of influences, or of affininities between Thackeray and St. Augustine, Shakespeare, Fielding, Fanny Burney, Dr. Johnson, Laclos, Goethe, Disraeli, Douglas Jerrold, Dickens, Trollope, Conan Doyle, and Evelyn Waugh.

Studies of *Vanity Fair* analyzing his wit, humor, irony, and mode of narration abounded, and yet they have been supplemented by more recent studies of his illustrations, manifold allusions, modes of composition, and the narrative's text. Perhaps the best way to epitomize the considerable body of modern critical responses to *Vanity Fair*—sometimes bewildering in their contradictions of each other—is to provide a brief statement of some of its important insights, all of which come from works found in the bibliography. John A. Lester's "Thackeray's Narrative Technique" (1954), for example, gave special attention to the narrator's freedom in moving backward and forward in time, to the variety of techniques that he employs to modify scenic and narrative presentation, and to the genius of the distinctly Thackerayan manner, which articulates the long view of human conduct made possible by retrospection, and by timeless moral insight. Lester's was the first essay ever devoted to his subject, and it remains unique.

Perhaps the most fundamental critical book on Thackeray remains Geoffrey Tillotson's *Thackeray the Novelist* (1954), which one can still recommend to readers of criticism as the place to begin their study. He finds Thackerayan unity to consist of what he calls a "oneness" of form and manner that produces a never-ending "flow" of "continuity," and he devotes considerable attention to Thackeray's use of the narrator (G. Tillotson, 11, 12, 20). Here, as with Lester, the scope of the analysis is broad, ranging as it does over a number of Thackeray's works. Kathleen Tillotson's *Novels of the Eighteen-Forties* (1954), however, includes a succinct chapter on *Vanity Fair* that emphasizes its serial nature, and the "firm planning and complex unity" that characterize its narrative (K. Tillotson, 225). A long introductory essay to the book provides a helpful historical context in which one can read *Vanity Fair*. The Tillotsons then wrote an excellent joint introduction (with notes) to what has remained the standard American paperback edition of the novel, published by Houghton Mifflin in 1963, and containing many of Thackeray's essential illustrations.

Other notable critical essays from the 1960s and thereafter include F. E. L. Priestley's insightful introduction to an edition of 1969, probably the best of such introductory essays; Sister Corona Sharp's "Sympathetic Mockery: A Study of the Narrator's Character in *Vanity Fair*" (1962), which helped to develop critical understanding of the narrator as a sophisticated ironist; and A. E. Dyson's *"Vanity Fair: An Irony against Heroes"* (1964). In fact, a concentration upon the narrator, in an attempt to achieve a more subtle understanding of his role and his significance, became a crucially important focus of intelligent critical effort during this period, as was illustrated also by Harriet Blodgett's essay, "Necessary Presence: The Rhetoric of the Narrator in *Vanity Fair*" (1967). A complementary effort to comprehend and articulate the coherence of Thackeray's narrative was furthered in a series of articles by Myron Taube, notably in "Contrast as a Principle of Structure in *Vanity Fair*" (1963), and by this author.

The major books published during this period included John Loofbourow's somewhat precious *Thackeray and the Form of Fiction* (1964), James Wheatley's somewhat restrained *Patterns in Thackeray's Fiction* (1969), Juliet McMaster's lively *Thackeray: The Major Novels* (1971), Barbara Hardy's sociologically oriented *Exposure of Luxury* (1972), Jack Rawlins's admiring and yet uncomfortably inhibited *Thackeray's Novels* (1974), John Sutherland's somewhat impressionistic *Thackeray at Work* (1974), Robert Colby's comprehensive *Thackeray's Canvass of Humanity* (1979), and perhaps Harden's compositionally oriented *Emergence of Thackeray's Serial Fiction* (1979). An important collection of reviews dating from 1840 through 1879 appeared in *Thackeray: The Critical Heritage,* edited by Geoffrey Tillotson and Donald Hawes (1968), which has been supplemented by bibliographies of Thackeray criticism edited by Dudley Flamm (1967), John Charles Olmsted (1977), and Sheldon Goldfarb (1989). More recently, Thackeray criticism has been augmented by a set of annotations to the selected works of Thackeray, including of course *Vanity Fair,* edited by this author (1990), and by the first modern edition of Thackeray's works, which has been begun under the general editorship of Peter Shillingsburg, who has edited the text of *Vanity Fair* (1989) cited in this book.

It is probably fair to say that any given reader's enjoyment of or discomfort with Thackeray's great narrative will depend to a significant degree upon his or her response to the narrator. However much modern critics have delighted in him and in his performance, or have narrowly and often pettishly complained when he expresses attitudes and values differing from their own, almost all have overtly or implicitly perceived the crucial artistic importance of this uniquely Thackerayan creation, and most have come indeed to see him as the central figure in Thackeray's masterpiece because he not only mediates the narrative to us, but also, with his recurrent metamorphoses and ambiguity of outlook, keeps us in the same state of uncertain awareness as his own. The recognition that we have been placed in this tantalizing position, moreover, may be one reason for this century's preeminent Thackeray scholar to have believed that in writing *Vanity Fair* Thackeray "gave to world literature one of those inexhaustible masterpieces which repay almost endless study."[32] This is the first substantial critical study ever devoted exclusively to *Vanity Fair,* and by means of its manner of presenting four different but complementary perspectives on Thackeray's masterful narrative, it is meant to suggest the possibilities of further investigation and understanding.

A READING

4

Expanding Panorama

As a poem is an active process, not a static object, so too is a novel, which is a linguistic process in the form of a narrative. We hold a physical book in our hands, but as we read we participate in the processive energies of the author's language as it renders for us a sequence of imaginatively perceived times, places, actions, characters, voices, and other vital aspects of narrative. Accordingly, this study of *Vanity Fair* seeks to evoke the dynamic energies of Thackeray's novel.

Because Vanity Fair *is* the world, we find ourselves immediately "Before the Curtain" of this particular booth in the fair, hearing the narrator address us directly. He is "Manager of the Performance," the Showman, who will unfold his narrative panorama before us. It begins in time: for the readers of 1847 a somewhat distant but still partly recoverable time, when "the present century was in its teens" (1); for us a time more remote and indistinct. With that opening phrase all readers, however, are immediately immersed in the most ambiguous of processes, for the present disappears even as we become aware of it and can be recaptured only intermittently and gradually with less and less success. *Time* crucially defines the world characterized by the

Preacher of Ecclesiastes as "under the sun"; time is the counterpart of the fundamental *placing* metaphor: the fair itself.

After its temporal opening, therefore, the first sentence places us in a setting marked by the precise details of *things:* "and on one sunshiny morning in June, there drove up to the great iron gates of Miss Pinkerton's academy for young ladies on Chiswick Mall, a large family coach with two fat horses in blazing harness, driven by a fat coachman in a three-cornered hat and wig, at the rate of four miles an hour." Here as hereafter we must be prepared to see that every word counts in this sentence, whose language is characterized by concreteness and specificity, as it conveys an image of wealth, physical well-being, and expansiveness, comically reflected in the sequence of two, three, four. By contrast, as the great iron gates and the subsequent ringing of the bell suggest, what we are about to see is a place of enclosure.

Miss Pinkerton's academy for young ladies is the first social institution to which the narrator introduces us. The "Chiswick dovecot" (2), as he comically terms it, is a sheltered environment where girls of prosperous and socially aspiring middle-class families are sent—ostensibly to be educated, but actually to learn greater polish and refinement of manners than their mothers could have taught them, and to emerge from the "academy" no longer as girls but allegedly as "young ladies" (1). In short, Miss Pinkerton's academy is an institution designed to assist social climbing. It therefore specializes in cultivating appearances, as we see in the narrator's richly amusing parody of schoolmistresses' letters to the purchasers of their services: Miss Pinkerton's "billet" (a word taken over from French to convey the impression of elegance).

This "billet," the first instance of formal social communication in the narrative, is a masterpiece of pretence, notable for its derangement of language. The first time we read the novel we will miss some of the letter's ironic comedy because we have not yet met the Sedley family, but as we read on, and especially as we give the novel its necessary second reading, we can much more adequately appreciate what the letter reveals. First of all, it sets out to flatter its recipient, Mrs. Sedley, into thinking that her home circle is "polished and refined" (1)—which it certainly is not. Even more, the letter employs language appropriately used only of an aristocratic lady, doing so in order to pretend that Amelia, like her parents, is a person of "birth and station" (1), which is completely untrue, given the humble origin of her parents. From the letter we also learn what the meager curriculum of the academy has been: Amelia has spent the last six years learning music, dancing, spelling, embroidery, needlework, and geography.

Quite revealingly, the letter places its greatest emphasis on the need for an appropriate *posture,* which is to be achieved by "a careful and undeviating use of the backboard . . . as necessary to the acquirement of that dignified *deportment and carriage* so requisite for every young lady of *fashion"* (1) (which, again, Amelia is not). The letter's final shallowness appears in its perfunctory mention of "the principles of religion and morality" (1), which serves only to introduce an allusion to Dr. Samuel Johnson, who once visited Miss Pinkerton, and whose visit she has turned by relentless advertisement into "the cause of her reputation and her fortune" (1). With that final phrase, which is the narrator's, we see revealed one of the crucial motives for posturing: to secure money.

Miss Pinkerton's, though governed by the deceptions of worldliness, is nevertheless a simple place. The ringing of the bell at its gate is enough to attract the attention of a score of heads; the wearing of a new waistcoat by Mrs. Sedley's coachman prompts notice by Miss Jemima; the making of a bouquet and sandwiches, and the gift of a recipe for making scented water are other major events of a day. From this very narrow confinement, then, the panorama of the narrative widens—widens with the repudiation of this boarding-school world. Both the posturing and the simplicity are rejected by Becky's startling, unforgettable act of throwing Johnson's *Dictionary* back into Miss Pinkerton's garden. Suddenly the posturing ends—for a moment— with this stunning ending of the opening narrative, an ending whose effect is reinforced by a full-page illustration, *Rebecca's Farewell.* Becky is not rejecting posturing in general, however, only that of *Miss Pinkerton,* since the "Dixonary" is an emblem of Miss Pinkerton's respectability and an advertisement for her school. Like all advertisement, it is posturing, but the *Dictionary* is also a gift from the simpleminded and warm-hearted Miss Jemima, and Becky is willing to cause her pain at this moment of departure, as the great gates close and the "world is before the two young ladies" (1).

We have learned about Amelia through the narrator's comments but also by seeing her in the social context of the school, where she has "twelve intimate and bosom friends out of the twenty four young ladies" (1), notably Miss Swartz, the mulatto heiress from St. Kitts, whom we shall see again, and the young orphan, Laura Martin, whom we shall not, but who is mentioned twice, whose wistful, affectionate language is quoted, and who seems to be depicted as the weeping girl in *Rebecca's Farewell*. Her prominence, however brief, and her wish to see Amelia as a surrogate mother suggest Amelia's warmth and maternal potential, which, as the narrator emphasizes, Becky so crucially lacks (2). In contrast to these emotional—indeed, comically excessive—*relationships,* we notice that Becky has only combative human *encounters* in chapter 1: the parting battle with Miss Pinkerton and the rejection of Miss Jemima's gift of the *Dictionary.*

The differences between the two girls are not only differences in emotional capacities and psychic proclivities, however. Another difference arises from external circumstances: "Miss Sedley's papa was a merchant in London and a man of some wealth; whereas Miss Sharp was an articled pupil" (1)—she has signed a contract whereby she provides her labor (teaching French) in exchange for the payment of school fees. People therefore treat them differently on the basis not only of the girls' different human natures, but also on the basis of their perceived wealth, or lack of it, and of the social position and prospects that it brings. We see this in the treatment they receive from Miss Pinkerton (though not from her sister), and most strikingly from the Sedley's black footman and coachman, who place in the carriage Amelia's flowers, presents, trunks, and bonnet-boxes, together with Becky's "very small and weatherbeaten old cow's-skin trunk . . . , the which was delivered by Sambo with a grin and packed by the coachman with a corresponding sneer" (1). Merely being employed by a wealthy family causes the footman and coachman to feel socially superior to someone they know only as impoverished.

As the girls ride from the suburb of Chiswick Mall toward the Sedley's house in Russell Square, a newly built area in west central

London inhabited especially by merchants and professional men, we learn about Becky's background as the orphan of a French opera-girl and a lazy, clever, drunken, dissolute English artist who lived in Soho, London's Bohemia. There, she developed "the dismal precocity of poverty" (2), learning to deal with the adult world, especially of males, and to discover her ability to play roles—a use of feigning and caricature that her isolation at Miss Pinkerton's helped develop into a habit. Hence we have some basis for comprehending her underlying rage and hatred, "her hard-heartedness, and ill-humour, and . . . her hostility to her kind" (2), but also her ability to understand herself as well as others: "I'm no angel" (2) is perhaps her most famous statement.

In reading the title of chapter 2, "In Which Miss Sharp and Miss Sedley Prepare To Open the Campaign," we may wonder what the "campaign" is. Most broadly it seems to mean the campaign of life, but by the end of the chapter we see that more immediately it means the campaign to secure a husband, and we understand why "Miss Sharp" has been given priority in the chapter title. After the years of school or private tutoring, marriage was the next major anticipated experience in a nineteenth-century young lady's life. Having learned that Amelia's brother is both rich and unmarried, Becky decides to open her campaign of husband-hunting against *him,* sight unseen.

When Becky enters the Sedley household she meets people of two different new worlds. First is the Anglo-Indian world of Jos Sedley, a bachelor of 29, who, in order to seek his fortune, joined the East India Company's civil service. As a member of this colonial enterprise, he has risen to the position of collector, "an honourable and lucrative post" (3) that involved collecting revenues for the company. His willingness to live in India for some eight years in spite of the unhealthiness of the Indian climate and the isolation of his post testifies to the zeal with which Jos and men like him sought their fortunes, which were often made quickly: in Jos's case, about eight years. "Luckily" (3), the narrator tells us, he caught a liver complaint that led to his returning on medical leave to London, where he makes a show of doctoring his complaint and pretends to be a Regency dandy, existing only for fashionable pleasure.

The other new world for Becky is that of the father of Jos and Amelia, John Sedley, characterized by the narrator as a "coarse man from the Stock Exchange" (3). Sedley is a self-made man active in the world of speculation and paper values. As we later see, he also speculates in commodities—and, like many speculators, ultimately crashes. For the present, however, which is still his time of financial success, Becky is especially struck by the material opulence of the household and by Amelia's material possessions: "Ah but to have parents as you have—kind, rich, affectionate parents who give you every thing you ask for. . . . My poor papa could give me nothing, and I had but two frocks in all the world!" (2). Mostly, of course, she is struck by the wealth of Jos, and her visit to the Sedley household takes its importance from her avid, flattering pursuit of him and from his amusing entanglement.

While Becky focuses her attention on Jos, the narrator, having introduced us to the world of a girls' boarding school, now takes us backward in time to introduce us to the world of a boys' boarding school. If Miss Pinkerton's academy was a sheltered dovecot, Dr. Swishtail's academy is a place of licensed violence, where the schoolmaster physically beats the students, where "every-day life" is characterized by "a big boy beating a little one without cause" (5), and where younger boys act as servants for the older boys, blacking their shoes, toasting their bread, retrieving their cricket balls, and running their errands—always under the duress of threatened violence. The school is also a place of intense snobbery among the boys (and evidently among their elders, like the usher), for these youngsters judge each other by the father's occupation or by conspicuous signs of wealth—the ownership of a carriage being a notoriously accepted qualification for being called a gentleman. Dobbin is the outsider here, being the son of a grocer and having his tuition and board paid for by delivery of his father's goods to the school. Only after getting the better of the school bully in a fistfight does he gain the approval of the other boys and feel sufficient confidence in himself to get what he can out of the Latin, mathematics, and French taught at the school—which, as the narrator clearly demonstrates, is another inept social and educational institution.

The world of public pleasure appears with the narrator's evocation of the gardens of Vauxhall and their entertainments, where members of different social classes met to enjoy the lights, the fiddlers, the pianists, the singers, the dances, the dark walks, and, if they can afford it, the suppers, the champagne, and, in Jos Sedley's unfortunate case, the rack punch. Here was another means of awakening the memories of *Vanity Fair*'s original readers, for, although the pleasure gardens still existed in 1847, their days of popularity had passed and their future was thought to be, and indeed was to be, short. In the narrative, Vauxhall Gardens thereby serve as an appropriate setting for comically demonstrating how Jos Sedley's inability to restrain his pursuit of pleasure helps to undermine Becky's efforts to extract a marriage proposal from him. The disappearing gardens also serve as a means of impressing upon readers the contingencies that circumscribe human plotting, and the evanescence of human life itself, with all its pleasures.

Becky's widening experience next comes to include a family that has a hereditary title and typical appurtenances: a country estate, a city mansion, and a seat in Parliament. (It actually controls two seats, but has economically rented one out for £1,500 a year.) Before she arrives in Great Gaunt Street, with its deathlike qualities, we readers are informed about the names in the family tree and what they reveal about this degenerate family and its history of groveling to try and secure the favor of whatever ruling faction is in power. The still-ignorant Becky, however, has illusions about the family because of its social status. The comedy of her meeting with her employer, Sir Pitt Crawley is therefore the comedy of failed expectations. Thinking that now, "at least, I shall be amongst *gentlefolks,* and not with vulgar [mercantile] people" (7), and expecting to see the baronet "very handsomely dressed in a court suit, with ruffles and his hair a little powdered" (7) she finds instead a vulgar, bald man in dirty, drab clothing—thereby raising again for readers the question of what it means to be a gentleman.

After a trip on the Southampton coach—another human institution whose transitoriness the narrator emphasizes—city-bred Becky's journey "into the wide world" (7) leads her to the repetitive life of a country estate, Queen's Crawley. Here she meets the second Lady

Crawley, an ironmonger's daughter who married for social position and whose spiritually empty life is epitomized by her action of "always knitting" an interminable piece of worsted (8). Sir Pitt "is always tipsy every night," and his son Pitt "always reads sermons in the evening" (8) and follows regular patterns of activities during the daytime, working in his study, riding to the local town on county business, or serving as a lay-preacher at a meetinghouse of worshippers independent of the Church of England, of which his uncle is an ordained rector.

Becky amusedly perceives the foibles of these people, whose attachment to the values of Vanity Fair reveals itself perhaps most clearly in the value that they attribute to money and position. Sir Pitt, "boor as he was," nevertheless "was a stickler for his dignity while at home, and seldom drove out but with four horses, and though he dined off boiled mutton had always three footmen to serve it" (9). Even more than Sedley, he is a speculator, buying granite mines, coal mines, and canal shares, horsing coaches, and taking government contracts, all the while dissipating his fortune with his speculations, his excessively sharp practices, and his interminable lawsuits. By greedily appropriating some of his son's legal inheritance, he has even given Pitt power over himself, so that an uneasy truce exists between them. Because they have no affection for each another, their relationship is determined solely by what the narrator calls "money arrangements." So it is in their relationship with Sir Pitt's unmarried elderly sister, Miss Crawley.

Serious issues emerge in the dialogue, as when Pitt asks a crucially important question: "What is money compared to our souls, Sir?" (10). The asking, however, seems tainted by self-justifying motives, as Sir Pitt indicates with his sardonic reply: "You mean that the old lady won't leave the money to you." Every potential heir in the family has but one thought regarding Miss Crawley, even the Rector (who holds the clerical living controlled by the family): "his great hope was in her death—when 'hang it' (as he would say), 'Matilda *must* leave me half her money'" (11). So here is another form of speculation, as the potential heirs engage in "these speculations in life and death."

Perhaps the most brilliantly amusing revelation of these grasping motives appears as the wife of the Rector gathers intelligence about Becky—at first, bland reports of the governess and the young ladies. "Then the report would come—The new governess be a rare manager—Sir Pitt be very sweet on her—Mr. Crawley too—He be reading tracts to her—'What an abandoned wretch!' said little, eager, active, black-faced Mrs. Bute Crawley." How could the *Rector's* wife interpret a willingness to listen to religious tracts as the sign of an unprincipled person unless she were also unprincipled and as knowledgeable as Becky about hypocrisy? And so that we should have no doubt about this matter, the narrator provides us with the comic spectacle of two polished hypocrites, Mrs. Bute Crawley and Miss Pinkerton, exchanging letters that communicate perfectly with one other, as the whole point of Mrs. Bute's letter, nominally camouflaged as a postscript, begets a responsive reply, similarly masked, as it provides what Mrs. Bute's letter implicitly sought: derogatory information about Becky's background, including hearsay about her mother, based on her mother's profession as an opera girl.

Becky's plotting is thus circumscribed again by the plotting of someone hostile to her, as in the earlier instance of George Osborne's plot to prevent her marriage to Jos Sedley. Becky contemptuously rejects an offer of marriage from a country surgeon, while Mrs. Bute schemes to entangle her with Rawdon, so that she will either be seduced and then discharged from her position, or so that she will snare Rawdon as a husband and thereby cause him to be disinherited by Miss Crawley. This formidable Rector's wife is more experienced in scheming than Becky, and more skilled in looking through Miss Crawley's pose as a freethinker and seeing the real snob beneath, who will reject Becky because of her family background, thereby enhancing Bute's chances at the elderly spinster's £70,000.

Amelia, on the other hand, seems quite safe "in the paternal nest," being matured by her love for George Osborne, "nor did it seem that any evil could befal her" (12). But her life too is being circumscribed—by large forces of which we begin to gain hints in chapter 12: the Napoleonic warfare that is sweeping Europe. Napoleon is a speculator on a large scale, staking his empire in the ventures of 1812–14: the invasion of Russia and burning of Moscow, the unsuccessful battle of Leipzig, and the minor victories against the invading Allied armies at Brienne and Montmirail, all of which agitate "all the hearts and all the Stocks of Europe," including of course those of that lesser speculator, John Sedley. With the abdication of Napoleon in April 1814 and his exile to Elba, George and Europe seem safe, but with Napoleon's return to France in March 1815, both are in jeopardy again, as is Amelia's engagement to George because "her father's fortune was swept down with that fatal news" (18) and because George's mercenary father has vowed to have "no lame duck's daughter in my family" (13).

Marriage constitutes the next widening of experience, first as Becky captures the younger son of a baronet, failing to pay sufficient attention to Lady Crawley's deteriorating health and thereby failing to anticipate how she might have had the baronet, who besides his title has an income of £4,000 a year. Indeed, few scenes of the narrative are more comical than the one in which Sir Pitt, in London on business, comes to see Becky, takes off "his black gloves and his hat with its great crape hat-band"—conventional, ostentatious semblances of mourning for his deceased wife, who has died only the previous day—proposes marriage to her, still holding his crepe hat, and finally goes down on his knees, only to hear Becky's anguished acknowledgment, "Oh, Sir—I—I'm *married already*" (14). Can't one call this a startling nineteenth-century instance of black comedy?

As a married woman Becky, of course, exhibits great dexterity. All too aware of Rawdon's mental deficiencies, she inwardly regrets that she cannot "make something of him" (17), but she shows him only pleasing attention, listening indefatigably to his boring stories, laughing at his jokes, and making a comfortable home for him: "she played and sang for him, made him good drinks, superintended his dinner, warmed his slippers, and steeped his soul in comfort." Clearly, she exists in isolation from her marital partner. For Amelia, however, marriage—at least at first—is a rescue from unhappy solitude. It begins with an "I will" that comes "fluttering up to her lips from her heart" (22), but is darkened by a meeting and a subsequent association with Becky and Rawdon at Brighton that soon produces unease in Amelia because she sees her trivial, self-indulgent husband, only a week after the wedding, becoming interested in Becky, who cannot resist practicing her charms upon him. The illustration, *A Family Party at Brighton* (25), perfectly captures the interplay of relationships: in the foreground George and Becky focused on each other; in the middle distance Rawdon winning money from Jos; and in the background the solitary figure of Amelia wistfully looking toward her husband. Solitude is precisely what she rediscovers in marriage.

Being the *younger* son of a baronet, Rawdon has no money. He and Becky therefore have to live on credit and on the money that Rawdon can win at billiards and cards from people who do have money, like Jos and especially George. The relationship is one of mutual parasitism, for the monetary disparity is counterbalanced by a social disparity. No matter how poor he is, Rawdon knows he is socially superior to people like Jos and George, and thinks and acts accordingly. Hearing the news of Old Sedley's catastrophe, he feels absolutely no sympathy, for he thinks of such people as "stockbrokers—bankrupts—used to it, you know" (17). When Dobbin appears in Brighton, because he has no vanity upon which Rawdon can play, "Crawley paid scarcely any attention to [him], looking upon him as a good-natured nincompoop, and under-bred city man" (25) [i.e. a man of mercantile background].

As for George, Rawdon easily takes his measure as a naïve young man who urgently wants to be seen with his social superiors: "He'd go to the deuce to be seen with a Lord. He pays their dinners at Greenwich, and they invite the company" (14). Most revealingly, when Miss Crawley asks whether George is "presentable," Rawdon replies, "Presentable?—oh, very well. You wouldn't see any difference." The difference exists, of course, and Rawdon's attitude is a mixture of contempt for George, and a delight in his own parasitic ability to draw blood from the wealthy merchant's son: "Hang those city fellows, they must bleed; and I've not done with him yet, I can tell you. Haw, haw!" It is at Brighton, therefore, that Becky and Rawdon establish their pattern of living upon credit, upon Rawdon's literal abilities as a gambler, and upon Becky's abilities to charm and entertain.

The panorama widens now to include Belgium, which the narrator ironically presents as the host country for foreign armies, especially the British, who pay their own way, and for British tourists who want to participate vicariously in the spectacle of war: "It was a blessing for a commerce-loving country to be overrun by such an army of customers: and to have such creditable warriors to feed. And the country which they came to protect is not military. For a long period of history they have let other people fight there" (28). These survivor hosts offer their guests great enticements, especially in Brussels, where all the Vanity Fair booths are laid out, bands are constantly playing, and life seems to be "a perpetual military festival." The English soldiers and tourists alike join in a life of illusion, emphasized by our historical knowledge of what is to come and by the narrator's pointed reminder that "Napoleon . . . was preparing for the outbreak which was to drive all these orderly people into fury and blood; and lay so many of them low."

In this foreign setting, rigid distinctions between middle-class people and their social superiors are somewhat relaxed, so that George is permitted to entertain the wife and daughter of a rather impecunious lord, as well as the lord himself. So, too, a social structure based upon military distinctions becomes quite prominent: being an aide-de-camp to General Tufto, Rawdon naturally associates with "two brilliant young gentlemen of fashion, who were, like himself, on the staff of a general officer" (29). Becky, of course, makes the most of her new social eminence, quite characteristically appearing with special brilliance at the Brussels opera house, where she acts not on the stage, like her mother, but in the audience.

Her greatest triumph, however, is at the unforgettable ball given the night before Waterloo, in the midst of which soldiers began discreetly to withdraw and to reassemble with their military units just before marching off to battle. Thackeray didn't have to invent this incident; it happened. From the "sound of revelry by night," in Byron's phrase, Wellington's officers marched off to the sound of cannon the next morning. As they marched they knew that the battle was not just another dance, but the night before they did not act as though they knew it. This scene of Becky's triumph, therefore, has a fundamental unreality about it, embodying as it does the thoughtless pursuit of pleasure up to the last possible moment. George's actions dramatize this folly most clearly as he gives Becky a note asking for an assignation, throbs "with triumph and excitement," goes off to a gambling table and bets "frantically," with a "trembling" hand asks to have his glass refilled, and then at the news of battle, with "a start and a wild hurray," drains his glass and walks off speedily to prepare for a battle from which he will not return.

The narrator has told us that Napoleon is "to perform a part in this domestic comedy of Vanity Fair" (18). But since it *is* a domestic comedy, his role is performed offstage and so is Waterloo and "the great game of war" (30). "Our place is with the non-combatants," as we watch the pathos of Amelia's suffering, the spectacle of Jos Sedley's farcical cowardice, and the maneuverings of Becky as she masterfully exploits his terror and as she contemptuously toys with the frantic Bareacres family—the same family that George Osborne had grovelingly entertained.

Part of the comedy centering on Jos depends upon our awareness of the thoughts and secret motives of his servant, Isidor, who looks upon Jos as his lawful prey, but who also has fantasies similar to those of Jos, especially as he imagines the power he will exert over other people by wearing gaudy clothing and ostentatious accouterments: Jos's frilled shirts, gold-laced cap, frogged frock coat, gold-headed cane, and the great double ring with rubies. Isidor works quite effectively upon Jos's fears, but even as he does so he proves himself to be fully as much immersed as Jos in the values of Vanity Fair. The same is true, of course, of Becky, who manipulates Jos even more effectively than Isidor.

One of the effects that comedy produces upon those who experience it, as Henri Bergson has pointed out, is a momentary anesthesia of the heart that accompanies laughter. This is precisely the effect that the little drama of Jos's fright produces upon Becky, and upon many readers as well. Perhaps the most uproarious moment in the entire novel occurs as Jos's ego-satisfying fantasies of himself as a military man all at once become terrifying. Having swaggered about in public for weeks with his new mustachios and military-style frogged coat, he comes to hear appalling rumors of a French victory at Waterloo, looks into a *mirror*, and, while still believing that his artifices are successful, abandons them pell-mell: "They *will* mistake me for a military man, thought he," frantically baring his neck, and calling upon Isidor (in incompetent French), "Cut me. Quickly! Cut me!" (32). When Isidor comes to understand that Jos desperately wants to have his mustachios shaved off (not to have his throat cut) and to have Isidor take away the military coat and cap, Isidor hears the words "with inexpressible delight"—a model for our response. Similarly, when Jos tries to justify his cowardly decision to flee Brussels by repeating an implausible rumor presumably invented by Isidor, Becky "enjoy[s] his perplexity." So do many readers, though of course to share in another person's enjoyment does not mean that we need approve of their motives.

Becky exploits Jos's terror while rejecting fear herself. After extorting an exorbitant sum of money from Jos for Rawdon's two horses, while keeping a mare for herself, she refuses to flee: "'Suppose the French do come,' thought Becky, 'what can they do to a poor officer's widow? Bah! . . . We shall be let to go home quietly, or I may live pleasantly abroad with a snug little income.'" The latter seems to her the more attractive alternative, buoyed by the fantasy of marrying a titled Frenchman. Rawdon survives, however, and so he and Becky enter a new world, passing the winter of 1815–16 in Paris spending the proceeds of the money paid for Rawdon's horses by Jos, who, now that he is off-stage, is sympathetically termed by the narrator "poor Jos Sedley" (34).

In Paris Becky achieves her greatest social success so far—partly because she speaks French so well and emulates the French ladies, adopting "at once their grace, their liveliness, their manner," but mostly because she skillfully uses Rawdon's relationship to old Miss Crawley to gain entrance into French society. The narrator reminds us that "all the world was at Paris during this famous winter" and so Becky had "a little European congress" around her, "who from her wit, talent, and energy, indeed merited a place of honour in Vanity Fair." He also, however, points out that no duns were pursuing Becky and Rawdon in Paris "as yet"—those two words making clear that the triumphs cannot last, having no permanent financial or any other basis.

Nevertheless, for the time being Becky and Rawdon's ability to survive financially in Paris for two or three years is explained in the famous Thackerayan chapters, "How To Live Well on Nothing A-Year" and "The Subject Continued." Becky achieves major new successes as a manager, rescuing Rawdon from the difficulties that his dubious tactics as a gambler cause him, deciding that their future lies in returning to England, where he might get a government appointment, and then successfully conducting the difficult negotiations with his English creditors to persuade them to accept ninepence or a shilling in the pound. Back in London, Rawdon and Becky attach themselves to a new creditor—that is, victim—Raggles, the former Crawley family servant. This time, however, the narrator tells us in advance the misery that they will cause their creditor, so that we view the subsequent narrative with knowledge of their callous behavior and its painful consequences for him and his family: "the poor wretch was utterly ruined by the transaction, his children being flung on the streets, and himself driven into the Fleet Prison" (37).

Living at a fashionable address, entertaining guests pleasantly, driving in Hyde Park, having a box at the opera, Becky establishes a successful but limited social position in London—not in "Society" but on its fringes. Her "wit, cleverness, and flippancy, made her speedily the vogue in London among a certain class," but "the ladies held aloof from her," recognizing that she is an adventuress—that is, a person who lives by scheming. Her conquest of fashionable, titled men serves as compensation, however, especially when the men include the Marquis of Steyne—not a mere baronet, but a peer of the realm. Steyne, of course, knows very well that Becky is an adventuress, but, unlike the women, he finds cynical amusement in her scheming as well as sexual attractiveness, his first response to Becky in the narrative being: "'Dear little innocent lamb . . . ,' said the Marquis; . . . and he began to grin hideously, his little eyes leering towards Rebecca."

Becky plans, first of all, to get herself entrance into society by having Lady Jane present her at Court—the king's acceptance of her being the supreme certification of her "respectability." Second, she wants to get Rawdon appointed to a paying government position so that they can have some income with which to keep creditors at bay. Hence her joy at the news of old Sir Pitt's death, as a result of which (and of her anticipated diplomacy with the new Sir Pitt), she sees the addded possibility of getting Rawdon into Parliament, occupying one

of the two seats that the Crawley family controls. Rawdon will therefore have added leverage in seeking his government appointment,
especially by allying himself in Parliament with Lord Steyne. This,
however, is just another of her fantasies.

Becky's return to Queen's Crawley helps us as well as her to
measure the growth of her experience and of her aspirations since she
first arrived as a penniless governess, though she has scarcely more
money or security now than she did then. Her illusions seem to have
grown along with her aspirations, for it seems to her "as if she was not
an impostor any more, and was coming to the home of her ancestors"
(41). Playacting throughout her visit, she pretends not only to the people at Queen's Crawley but also to herself, "as if there were not cares
and duns, schemes, shifts, and poverty, waiting outside the Park gates,
to pounce upon her when she issued into the world again."

This behavior and these narrative comments help form the context for interpreting Becky's famous remark: "I think I could be a good
woman if I had five thousand a year." On the surface, her remark has
some plausibility: £5,000 a year *would* relieve her of poverty. But how
could money make Becky *good?* Given her amoral nature, her schemes
would presumably just take a different form and her pleasure in mocking, defying, and deceiving other people would continue. Becky's fantasy notion of leading a "good" life seems to be limited to ordering
half-a-crown's worth of soup for the poor and going to church, "if I
only had practice," she says, thereby thinking again in terms of performance and forgetting about the necessary inner motivation of charity.
Confined within these illusions, she concludes with a circular statement: "I could pay everybody, if I had but the money." As the narrator
remarks, she is offering herself consolation: "Becky consoled herself by
so balancing the chances and equalising the distribution of good and
evil in the world." His language, as we see, ironically uses metaphors
of commerce, as though good and evil can be measured and distrib-
uted.

The narrator's chief metaphor in chapter 41 for *avoidance,* however, grows out of the literal fact of everyone's avoiding the dark cof-
fin in which old Sir Pitt lies, awaiting burial. By avoiding the fact of
death, as everyone in the house does, these people are avoiding the

fact of living "beneath the sun"—that crucial awareness that, as we have seen, provides humans with their most fundamental understanding of themselves and their condition. Because the new Sir Pitt, for example, avoids the confrontation with death, he avoids important moral responsibilities in life—like those to his brother. As the narrator points out, "morally he was Rawdon's debtor" (44), but "the mere sense of [being in the] wrong makes very few people unhappy in Vanity Fair" (41).

The panorama expands to include a military station in India, but does so only briefly to show how Dobbin and Glorvina "were each exemplifying the Vanity of this life, and each longing for what he or she could not get" (43). The loneliness that this implies—seen already in the lives of Amelia, of Old John Sedley, lost in his fruitless economic schemes, of Old Osborne, trapped in his bullying rage and unforgivingness, of Jane Osborne, sitting alone in mirrored emptiness—now is seen to characterize both Rawdons as well. If the boy has lost even his illusion of having a real mother, his father, having previously dwindled from Colonel Crawley into "Mrs. Crawley's husband" (37), has now been beaten "and cowed into laziness and submission" (45). At least, however, as a result they discover a human resource in each other and especially in Lady Jane and her children. Amelia, of course, has already found compensation in young George—even to excess, for the child has become "her being" (35), which is thereby threatened when she has to give him up to Old Osborne.

Meanwhile, Becky mounts to the pinnacle of society, presentation at court, where she enters into the vacuous presence of George IV, after which, having been certified as "respectable," she gains entry to the social eminence of Lord Steyne's "town palace" (47), the significantly named Gaunt House. The whole scene of the court presentation is darkly comical as Sir Pitt, with his sword between his legs, comes with Lady Jane in a great carriage to Becky's house, "to the edification of Raggles" (48)—a self-victimizer as well as victim—and as Rawdon comes in a shabby old Guards' uniform that is much too tight, while Becky appears in stolen lace and in diamonds secretly given her by Sir Pitt and by Lord Steyne. Since "to be, and to be thought, a respectable woman was Becky's aim in life," she comes at times to believe in the role she is playing, and rides to court having "adopted a demeanour so grand, self-satisfied, deliberate, and imposing, that it made even Lady Jane laugh." "But the finest sport of all after her presentation was to hear her talk virtuously." Here again her role-playing clouds her awareness of her real nature and conduct.

Even Lord Steyne cannot prompt her to understand the folly of her aspirations. First, he gives her practical advice, telling her that "You won't be able to hold your own [in the great social world], you silly little fool. You've got no money." Even with a government appointment, Becky and Rawdon will be poor compared with the people whom she wants to emulate and with whom she wants to associate. Then Steyne makes a far more devastating comment. Ironically, it is this cynical, worldly man, thoroughly committed to the values of Vanity Fair, who, of all the characters we meet, delivers the most telling criticism of it: "Everybody is striving for what is not worth the having!"

Supplementing Steyne's observation is the narrator's emphasis on the illumination that an awareness of the passing of time can bring and how it calls into fundamental question the value of worldly pursuits. We see the unreality of attempting to ignore time in the image of Rawdon having forced himself into the old and shabby Guards' uniform of his youth, in the startlingly comic image of a someone who actually *has* a fine social position, a "stout countess of sixty, *décolletée*, painted, wrinkled, with rouge up to her drooping eyelids, and diamonds twinkling in her wig," and in the image of the apparently impoverished Lady Castlemouldy, suddenly revealed with "all the chinks and crannies with which time has marked her face." We also see the changed perspective that time brings in the instance of Becky's court dress, which, "if you were to see it now, any present lady of Vanity Fair would pronounce it to be the most foolish and preposterous attire ever worn," a onetime "milliner's wonder [that has] . . . passed into the domain of the absurd, along with all previous vanities."

So too, when Becky finally enters Gaunt House, the first guests about whom we learn are Lady Bareacres, an inspiration for Canova in her lovely youth, but "a toothless, bald, old woman now—a mere rag of a former robe of state" (49), and her husband, "a withered, old, lean man." Subsequently, great doors are opened for her, but the narrative of her "aristocratic pleasures" begins with the reader's being told that "these too, like all other mortal delights, were but transitory" (51)—quite transitory, in fact, because Becky's "success excited, elated, and then bored her" and because the period of her "success" is quite short. Its high point comes in the most appropriate of settings for Becky: a charade theater in Gaunt House, where we witness one of Thackeray's most brilliant scenes, as Becky plays the contrasting parts of Clytemnestra and Philomèle, in the latter role tellingly dressed as a marquise.

In spite of his warnings to Becky, Steyne avidly indulges *his* folly. Having previously superintended the departure of young Rawdon and Briggs, he arranges to have Rawdon arrested by bailiffs on the very night of Becky's success at charades so that he can have a subsequent evening alone with her and presumably collect a sexual reward. He knows, of course, the kind of person with whom he is dealing, but his cynicism delights in her accomplished dishonesty and, characteristically, he expresses his insight with great directness: "What an accomplished little devil it is! . . . What a splendid actress and manager! . . . She is unsurpassable in lies!" (52). Steyne, however, like Becky, indulges in the arrogant fantasy that his manipulations can be sustained indefinitely—until Rawdon demonstrates otherwise.

Becky's deceptiveness seems to express itself with extraordinary ease, but the terrible strain of constantly needing to perform becomes evident in two striking ways. The first awareness that we gain of what is going on beneath her lively surface occurs when little Rawdon creeps downstairs to hear Becky singing to Steyne in her drawing room, the door of which suddenly opens to reveal "the little spy" (44)—a telling word that helps to account for her impulsive reaction. "His mother came out and struck him violently a couple of boxes on the ear." When her performance is suddenly and unexpectedly interrupted, she erupts in rage and with violence. Steyne, not surprisingly, is amused by her "artless" behavior. The other revelation occurs not on a single occasion, but rather when the narrator identifies a recurrent relaxation of her controlled features when Rawdon falls asleep in his chair after dinner: "he did not see the face opposite to him, haggard, weary, and terrible; it lighted up with fresh candid smiles when he woke. It kissed him gaily" (52). The word *it*, suggesting an almost disembodied face, powerfully conveys the ghastly effort required to maintain her role, and the word *candid* brilliantly articulates the narrator's ironic ability to express the duplicity of her motives.

During the great discovery scene when Rawdon comes home from confinement for debt to find the servants sent away and Becky entertaining Steyne, even *she* cannot manage to act her way out of this compromising situation, though after giving a faint scream she makes a brief attempt: "she tried a smile, a horrid smile, as if to welcome her husband" (53). Her only other response is to repeat the words "I am innocent," causing the reader of course to wonder: "innocent of what?" Even as she utters the phrase and takes hold of Rawdon's coat and hands, we see that her own hands are covered with jewels and her arms with coiling bracelets, literally and suggestively called "serpents." Steyne, the nerves of whose mouth twitch "as he tried to grin at the intruder," bluntly denies her claim, basing his response on the fact that he has given her jewels and money, for which, Steyne imagines, she has been "sold" by Rawdon. (We know that Rawdon has not been involved; therefore, she has "sold" herself.) Steyne bases his other denial of her "innocence" by likening her to her mother, "the ballet-girl," whose profession, as we have previously seen, gave individual girls the reputation—sometimes justifiable, sometimes not—of being sexually for sale. Finally, we learn that Becky's maid has been "her accomplice and in Steyne's pay." Accomplice for what purpose?

In short, we are prompted by the details of the scene to *ask questions,* and the narrator only offers more of them: "What *had* happened? Was she guilty or not? She said not; but who could tell what was truth which came from those lips; or if that corrupt heart was in this case pure?" Even in the midst of defeat she can approve of Rawdon's violent attack on Steyne and "admire . . . her husband, strong, brave, victorious," so that our judgment, like the narrator's, must recognize her remarkable abilities and well as her profound corruption: "All her lies and her schemes, all her selfishness and her wiles, all her wit and genius had come to this bankruptcy"—another brilliantly chosen word that expresses an emotional as well as a moral and financial bankruptcy. Other characters like Sir Pitt and Macmurdo accept or pretend to accept the verdict of Becky's innocence, but Rawdon refuses to do so, saying: "If she's not guilty, Pitt, she's as bad as guilty" (55). That statement, too, is puzzling, however. What does it mean to be "as bad as guilty"? Rawdon's statement and his "broken and sad" condition suggest that he too is morally and emotionally as well as financially bankrupt—a judgment that is confirmed by his acceptance of the governorship of Coventry Island, where he goes to face isolation and the high probability of early death.

Because a similar bankruptcy characterizes the life of Old Sedley, Amelia feels forced to surrender young George to his Osborne grandfather, who, though financially opulent, heads a household of moral and emotional penury. George, having been brought up by a "weak mother, so tremulous and full of sensibility" (46), soon comes to dominate her and to become quite self-centered. Living with her in financially straitened circumstances, he becomes attracted to signs of wealth, getting "immense pleasure," for example, from the carriage of the Misses Dobbin "and its splendours" (38). When he comes to live with Old Osborne, therefore, he revels in the comfort and luxury that his grandfather provides for him, and grows more and more to be like his egoistic, dandified father. His idea of a gift for his mother is a miniature portrait of *himself*, and when he writes an essay "On Selfishness," he seems to have no notion of its applicability to himself, nor does she.

With the return of Jos and Dobbin from India, the Sedleys and Amelia are rescued from their narrow circumstances, but the ensuing deaths of the Sedleys prompt from the narrator a remarkable meditation on the central arch and stairwell of a London house, from which perspective one can observe a microcosmic world "of Life, Death, and Vanity" (61). Addressing the reader as "my friend in motley," he alludes to the title page illustration showing a congregation of motleyed fools listening to a similarly dressed and similarly natured speaker, and he directs our attention to the crucial future event in all our lives: "Your comedy and mine will have been played then, and we shall be removed, O how far, from the trumpets, and the shouting, and the posture-making." Those people like Old Osborne who are briefly left behind, however, continue the posture-making, pretending to themselves that their good fortune comes from "merit and industry, and judicious speculations" (making him a counterpart of Becky and many others), and that being a "better" man means only having more money: "[Sedley] was a better man than I was, this day twenty years— a better man I should say, by ten thousand pound"—to the utter degradation of the meaning of the core word *good*.

A final geographical widening of the panorama occurs when Dobbin, Jos, Amelia, and young George travel to Pumpernickel, another microcosm of Vanity Fair. Here the absurdities of life are seen in comical miniature and in utter transparency. Everyone knows everyone else, the foreign secretary lives over a pastry shop, the palace is incomplete from want of money, and the army consists of many officers, a few men, and a band. The major event of the summer is of course a fair and at one of its gambling tables, not surprisingly, we meet Becky, masked, wearing a low-cut, somewhat soiled dress, and unsuccessfully wagering a couple of florins at roulette.

Her reappearance allows the narrator to give us a brief overview of the seamy life of an English expatriate wandering on the continent—doing so with the indirectness that he feels his contemporary audience requires of him. He therefore elaborately characterizes her as a siren in order to convey her metaphoric cannibalism, as she lives off of other people, sucking out their generosity, their credulity, and even their cynicism. Tracing the gradual despondency and degradation of this "very vain, heartless, pleasure-seeking" (64) individual, he sketches her life from Boulogne to Dieppe, Caen, Tours, Paris, Brussels, and then a host of cities elsewhere in France, Germany, and Italy—at first alone, then with other women, sometimes respectable, sometimes not, and finally with men like the revealing-named Major Loder, who freeloads at fashionable entertainments and cheats at games of chance with extra cards and presumably with loaded dice.

At first she stays at hotels and then boarding houses and *pensions,* being addicted to society, no matter what kind. In one of his most essentially defining statements the narrator says: "Becky loved society, and, indeed, could no more exist without it than an opium-eater without his dram." At first also she tries strenuously to create the appearance of respectability and orderliness, "but the life of humdrum virtue grew utterly tedious to her." She begins to drink in her room, to gamble nightly, and to associate with disreputable people, whom the narrator politely characterizes as "Bohemians": "her taste for disrespectability grew more and more remarkable. She became a perfect Bohemian ere long," going about from town to town with them, where of course they seek the only income available to them: winnings, whether honest or dishonest, from gambling—the activity in which she is engaged when we come to see her in Pumpernickel. Perhaps the most comical image of her disorderly life is conveyed by the scene when Jos calls at the Elephant Hotel, where in a room littered with her clothing she receives him, after putting a rouge pot, a brandy bottle, and a plate of partly eaten sausage *into* her bed under the covers, and then sitting on top of them.

When she is taken up by Amelia and finds herself again in comfortable surroundings, her habits moderate, as she welcomes the change in her life. Her major contribution, however, is an unwitting one: her mere presence causes the quarrel between Amelia and Dobbin that ultimately permits them to reestablish their relationship upon new and better terms—without requiring the help that Becky belatedly offers: the evidence of George's note to her. With Jos her role is more threatening, but—as on a number of previous occasions in the narrative—not completely knowable.

Jos himself is a contradictory witness, terming her "innocent" (her earlier repeated word for herself) but also "terrible" (67). The full-page illustration, *Becky's second appearance in the character of Clytemnestra* offers an indirect statement, but it may simply dramatize her wish, not her deed, and is no more conclusive evidence than the fact that her solicitors, Messrs. Burke, Thurtell, and Hayes, have the same names as well-known murderers. Instead of being melodramatically murderous, Becky's relationship to Jos seems rather to be metaphorically cannibalistic, for she lives upon his wealth, has him take out a life insurance policy naming her as one of the beneficiaries, and—indulging her passion for gambling—has him engage in financial speculations that ultimately dissipate the remainder of his wealth.

In contrast to Becky's destructive cannibalism (a metaphor overtly used in chapter 64), we note Amelia's final relationship with Dobbin, which the narrator inevitably sees as one of fond but clinging dependence, and of new but presumably limited growth: "Grow green again, tender little parasite, round the rugged old oak to which you cling!" As he had said long before, "I think it was her weakness which was her principal charm:—a kind of sweet submission and softness, which seemed to appeal to each man she met for his sympathy and protection" (38). Both Amelia and Becky, then, finally find themselves living amid mixed conditions of life: Amelia in a gentle but emotionally flawed marriage, and Becky in a strenuously maintained position as the respectable "Lady Crawley" in the society of several provincial spas. If Becky has achieved her booth in Vanity Fair, Amelia, Dobbin, George, and Jane find themselves merely on the other side of the counter, as the ironic full-page illustration, *Virtue rewarded; A booth in Vanity Fair,* shows. In the world of Vanity Fair, how could it be otherwise? In such a world, determined corruption may well achieve a "status" similar to or even superior to that of flawed goodness. But the inherent fallacy in the psychology of human desire will always reveal itself in dismaying triumph over everyone, whether he or she seeks to do good or evil: "Ah! *Vanitas Vanitatum!* Which of us is happy in this world? Which of us has his desire? or, having it, is satisfied?"

5

Emerging Serial

For the novelist who wrote *Vanity Fair,* as we saw in chapter 1, serial composition meant the necessity of meeting 19 successive monthly deadlines in order to produce 32 pages of text (64 for the final double number), together with two full-page illustrations and a varying number of smaller illustrations that initiated each chapter and that also appeared as insets and occasionally as tailpieces. Thinking of this jointly enhancing relationship of the author's pen and his drawing pencil, Thackeray gave the narrative its original subtitle: "Pen and Pencil Sketches of English Society." The subtitle also indicates that the narrative's purpose is to unfold the complex interrelationships comprising a society: the expanding panorama that we saw in chapter 4.

The guiding principle of *Vanity Fair*'s development as a serial narrative, therefore, is not so much a causal arrangement of effects, as it is a presentation of analogous and contrasting relationships among characters and among revealingly archetypal situations—a presentation that indicates careful planning and an intricate linking of details, both within separate monthly numbers and also in successive monthly numbers. As readers of these 19 installments of the narrative, we experience endings that are not endings, but that are instead temporary moments of rest in a continuing process. As readers also we come more and more to recognize the varied reenactments of earlier experience, and thereby to understand more fully the coherence of the narrative.

As the first serial number opens, with its evocation of the little world of Miss Pinkerton's Academy, we experience comical and sometimes startling contrasts of personality and situation, especially between Miss Barbara Pinkerton and her sister, and between Becky and Amelia. The relationship between the Pinkerton sisters seems to establish at the very outset a prototype of dominance and acquiescence, as Miss Barbara exerts control and Jemima admires and obeys. The former has her emotions, like her language, under strict control, while the simple, uncalculating Jemima expresses herself straightforwardly. We see her capacity for kindness and generosity, but she expresses these emotions tremblingly and blushingly. When her sister forcefully rejects Jemima's timid suggestion that Becky be given a copy of Johnson's *Dictionary*, Jemima, feeling "exceedingly flurried and nervous" (1), surprisingly asserts herself by giving Becky the *Dictionary* in spite of the prohibition. Becky's defiant refusal to accept the gift, therefore, exists in striking comic juxtaposition with Jemima's singular act of defiance of authority in offering it.

The personalities and situations of Becky and Amelia, however, naturally form the chief contrast at the opening of the narrative. The fact that Becky has come from a poor, Bohemian, somewhat disreputable background, with a clever but dissolute widowed father, does not nearly account for the difference in personality between herself and Amelia, who comes from a nearly opposite background. Much more, the difference derives from Amelia's open, emotional nature: "such a kindly, smiling, tender, gentle, generous heart of her own, as won the love of everybody who came near her"—except, presumably, Becky, who as we later learn doesn't even love her own son. Becky seems incapable of loving anyone else, and so the indifference with which she is treated at the school contrasts with Amelia's popularity. "I hate the whole house" (2), she says in a fury, prompting the narrator to call her a misanthropist, who "never was known to have done a good action in behalf of anybody."

Having learned of Jos Sedley's wealth and unmarried status, Becky determines to catch him, the comedy arising of course from the fact that *he* is the one who is exceedingly shy and easily flurried, while she pretends to be timid, demure, and submissive, praising his personal appearance and pretending an interest in things Indian, dropping her handkerchief twice for him to pick up for her, performing at the piano, displaying apparently heartfelt feeling, gently squeezing his hand, praising Hessian boots, and, most memorably, entangling him in a web of green silk that she is using to make—what else?—a *purse*. By contrast, George Osborne is lovingly drawn to Amelia by her expression of sympathetic emotion for Becky, while Amelia herself, "in the most unaffected way in the world, put[s] her hand into Mr. Osborne's" (4), as they walk into the back drawing room. Jos's vanity is, of course, utterly flattered by the actions of the only young lady who has ever shown an interest in him other than the Miss Cutler whom he constantly mentions, his grotesque misreading of the game of dominance and submission expressing itself in the wonderful comic misstatement: "It's evident the poor devil's in love with me"—not "lucky girl," but "poor devil," the alleged victim of his charms. Jos's statement is a brilliantly realized Thackerayan insight into our human ability (even propensity) to deceive ourselves.

In reading the second serial installment, we see at the outset how the principles of parallelism and contrast operate between adjacent numbers, as the world of Dr. Swishtail's Academy for Young Men recalls Miss Pinkerton's Academy for Young Ladies. At Dr. Swishtail's the most popular boy, Cuff, is also the most domineering, while the most unpopular is the acquiescent Dobbin, who responds to everyone's mockery by being "entirely dumb and miserable" (5), unlike Becky, who privately rages and makes plans for the future. The metaphoric "battle" (1) between Miss Pinkerton and the rebellious, self-possessed Becky finds a literal counterpart early in the second installment as Dobbin rebels against the injustice of "a big boy beating a little one without cause" (5) and therefore fights Cuff—at first quivering with nervousness and rage, and then becoming "as calm as a Quaker" (5). Like Becky, he triumphs over a domineering bully, but unlike her of course he acts, at least partly, to shield another person.

The famous ending of chapter 1 also finds a contrasting counterpart in chapter 5. Whereas Becky forcefully rejects Jemima's kind if naïve gift of the *Dictionary,* Dobbin accepts Cuff's magnanimous help, advances in self-esteem and academic ability, and ends by receiving a prize book in Becky's "mother tongue" (2). Being rewarded by his father with two guineas, he generously spends most of it on a general feast for his schoolfellows.

With the conclusion of this retrospective passage about the schoolboy world that also serves to introduce Dobbin and George, we return to the present. If the middle portion of the first serial number depicts the beginning of Becky's campaign to capture Jos, its counterpart in the second number depicts the unsuccessful conclusion of her campaign. Both portions begin with coach rides—the first to Russell Square, during which we learn about Becky's past, including her attempt to ensnare the Reverend Mr. Crisp, and the second to Vauxhall Gardens, during which we participate in various speculations about her future with Jos. After arriving at the Sedley house and being given a tour of the house, as well as presents and evidence that Jos is a wealthy bachelor, Becky had silently resolved at the end of the second chapter to catch him. Now in chapter 6, touring the gardens with Jos, she tries but fails to draw a proposal of marriage out of him. His shyness cannot be overcome except by a quantity of rack punch, where his self-indulgence leads to drunkenness—thereby saving him, ironically, from becoming her victim.

Old Sedley's mocking of his son in chapter 3 arises from a contempt for Jos's pretentions to be a man of fashion. George Osborne's mocking of Jos in chapter 6, however, reveals motives much more selfish and mean-spirited, because George not only exhibits a pompousness as great as Jos's but also a snobbishness that exceeds anything in Jos's behavior: rejecting Becky as a potential sister-in-law because she is a governess. Old Sedley, who likes to ridicule other people, bursts into coarse laughter at Becky's discomfiture at eating unexpectedly fiery curry and chili, but she quickly and effectively regains her poise in that situation. Jos Sedley, by contrast in chapter 6, racked by the pain of a hangover and by the acute embarrassment of hearing George Osborne's mockery of him, remains in bed all day and then rushes out of town seeking to escape from the witnesses of his performance at Vauxhall. Here again we recognize a contrasting serial reenactment, for we saw him shyly tiptoe out of his father's house in Russell Square at the end of chapter 3 to avoid seeing Becky, thereby causing a temporary setback in her campaign. Now, however, his flight is anguished and desperate; it ensures, moreover, that *she* will have to leave Russell Square as well, and assume the occupation of a governess rather than that of a wife.

The final chapter of the second serial number introduces Becky to a new family, one that is socially higher than the Sedleys, but also unexpectedly less opulent in its style of living. Sir Pitt Crawley, literally a dirty old man—and, as we later discover, figuratively as well—is another coarse jester, like Old Sedley, but one whose penurious manner of living comically contrasts with that of the prosperous merchant of Russell Square, for Sir Pitt drinks beer rather than champagne and eats a meager supper of tripe and onion at the same table as his housekeeper. Instead of enjoying a cheerful evening in Russell Square, as in chapter 4, with good food, music, and pleasant social conversation with Amelia, George, and especially Jos, who tells her long stories about India, Becky finds herself in chapter 7 in gloomy Great Gaunt Street listening to Sir Pitt's long sequence of confidences—in which, however, she also finds amusement. She had failed to elicit a proposal from Jos at the end of chapter 4, but he had vowed to make the proposal at Vauxhall. Now, in chapter 7, at the parallel moment in the second number, she responds to his failure to do so by dreaming about a new quarry, the Crawley son in the red military jacket, thereby preparing for her entrance into Queen's Crawley, and into a new web of circumstances.

The third serial number focuses entirely upon Queen's Crawley, beginning with Becky's amused and satirical perspective on its inhabitants, as expressed in her letter to Amelia, and then continuing from the perspective of the narrator, who shows us the interrelationships among the three chief inhabitants, and the responses of Lady Crawley and Pitt to the dominance of Sir Pitt, characterized by the narrator as a "cunning, mean, selfish, foolish, disreputable old man" (9). Rose Dawson, the local ironmonger's daughter who sold herself into mar-

riage with Sir Pitt, has become socially isolated and spiritually bankrupt as a result; hence she functions as "a mere machine in her husband's house," which she apparently never leaves, her most
characteristic act being the mechanical, endless knitting of pieces of
worsted. By contrast, Pitt responds to the coarseness of his father by
trying to impose conventions of polite behavior on the household and
by reading sermons at night while his father gets drunk with the butler.
Pitt's resolute acting in the role of "a very polite and proper gentleman," moreover, is successful enough to make his father stand "in awe
of him"—not sufficiently in awe to pay his son what he owes him from
his mother's legacy—but enough to moderate his behavior in Pitt's
presence. As the narrator ironically observes, "Sir Pitt never swore at
Lady Crawley while his son was in the room."

The controlling importance of money in governing the relationship of father and son also manifests itself in the relationship of Sir
Pitt's sister to Pitt and Rawdon, and of Bute to his brother and sister.
Both sets of brothers engage in the archetypal struggle of brothers in
Vanity Fair: "silent battles for reversionary spoil" (11). Pitt knows that
his aunt despises him and intends to leave half of her money to
Rawdon, but instead of being satisfied with his own position as his
father's heir and pleased at Rawdon's good fortune, he expresses his
frustrated greed by condemning his brother as well as his aunt, who,
however, clearly sees his hypocrisy. Bute the clergyman and his brother, Sir Pitt, engage in a different form of hypocrisy, for although they
"hate each other all the year," they forsake quarreling during Miss
Crawley's visits for fear of offending her.

Becky's relationship to members of the family, however, receives
primary narrative attention at the close of the third serial installment.
We see her becoming increasingly important to Sir Pitt, serving as his
secretary and confidante, in fact acting almost as mistress of the house
when Pitt is absent. Having become "quite a different person from the
haughty, shy, dissatisfied little girl" (10) of a year or so previously, she
has become more adept at practicing a "system of hypocrisy." She also,
of course, ingratiates herself with Pitt, thereby increasing Mrs. Bute's
anxiety, causing the latter to seek damaging information about Becky
from Miss Pinkerton, and then to establish a counterplot by promoting

Becky's association with Rawdon during Miss Crawley's visit. They hardly need encouragement, however, as Rawdon pursues Becky, and as she merrily rejects his improper advances, but also enticingly takes a puff on his cigar—thereby prompting Sir Pitt's furious sexual jealousy. The chapter and serial number then end with the narrator's cleverly ambiguous promise that Becky will be "a match . . . for father and son too"—a promise that looks ahead directly to the ending of the fourth serial number and, contrastingly, with that of number 5 as well.

The fourth installment concentrates on Amelia before returning at the end to Becky's relationships with members of the Crawley family. Whereas Becky had settled in at Queen's Crawley and begun to make a place for herself at the opening of the previous installment, Amelia by contrast in number 4 finds herself alone and rejected by the young ladies with whom she associates. Instead of being the popular girl that she was at Miss Pinkerton's, she now is the subject of female jealousy, especially from the Misses Osborne and the Misses Dobbin, who are reacting against the fondness that their brothers feel toward her. Becky would presumably have responded with covert satirical amusement and untiring overt flattery and attentiveness, as she does at Queen's Crawley, but Amelia finds their condescension and patronizing manners to be unsettling and their dullness to be what it is: boring. Precisely those qualities that attract men are what these pompous unmarried women find objectionable: her sweetness, freshness, artlessness, tenderness, domesticity, and submissiveness.

In her isolation, Amelia understandably centers her life in George—unfortunately, however, magnifying her image of him with "idolatry and silly romantic ideas" that make him seem like "a Fairy Prince," while diminishing her image of herself into that of "a humble Cinderella" (12). The dominant figure in this portion of the narrative, therefore, becomes George. Responding to his sisters' telling him that he is throwing himself away upon Amelia, he "gave himself up to be loved with a good deal of easy resignation." Being worshiped by Amelia, he says: "I adore her and that sort of thing" (13). Being a subject of hero worship by younger members of his military company, he plays the role of a man of the world who has more wild oats to sow before he can consent to be married. Even though Dobbin intervenes on Amelia's behalf, as he will crucially do later, and lends George money to buy a present for Amelia, the sight of a diamond shirt pin in a jeweler's window with which he can adorn himself soon obliterates any idea of a present for her.

The depiction of relationships between fathers and sons extends itself to number 4 with the appearance of Old Osborne. We have seen how Old Sedley despises his financially independent son for being "vain selfish lazy and effeminate" (6) and how Sir Pitt feels sexually jealous of Rawdon and feels a certain awe for Pitt, to whom he owes money. In Old Osborne we see a tyrannical, yet free-spending father who uses his financially dependent son to have vicarious experiences of his own, as he imagines that his monetary allowances enable his son to be "living in the best society in England" (13). A mixture of a toady and a bully, he grovels before his social superiors and sacrifices his children to fulfill the wishes of his own ego, as the Iphigenia clock emblemizes. For him, marriage being a commercial transaction, Amelia's suitability for his son is undermined by indications of Old Sedley's financial difficulties. Refusing to recognize his own moral and financial indebtedness to Old Sedley, who gave him his start, Old Osborne makes the marriage contingent upon Sedley's payment of Amelia's promised £10,000 dowry. Sedley, however, fails even to get a loan and therefore is assured of bankruptcy, while George, by contrast, succeeds in flattering his father's illusions, thereby getting a substantial new allotment of cash.

In the final chapter of number 4, as the narrative shifts back to Becky and the Crawleys, the relationships between father and son as well as between aunt and nephew develop with a new intensity. While Lady Crawley becomes terminally ill but receives little notice from the household, the minor illness of Miss Crawley attracts avid attention from Rawdon and from his father, driven by sexual jealousy of each other as rivals for Becky, who attends her. Meanwhile, Mrs. Bute, hoping of course for Rawdon's portion of Miss Crawley's legacy, fans Rawdon's jealousy. When Becky returns with Miss Crawley to London, the association between Becky and Rawdon leads to the secret marriage that represents her gamble with her future. The ending of the previous serial number with the promise that Becky would be a match for father and son leads pointedly to the conclusion of number 4, where Sir Pitt proposes to Becky only to learn that she has married already; number 5 will reveal that her husband is his son.

Number 5 traces her efforts to secure Miss Crawley's approval, the inevitable failure of those efforts, and the contrasting fortunes of Amelia. Becky has had a year or so to develop her "system of hypocrisy" (10), but has not yet managed to see through a different "system" like that of Miss Crawley, who pretends to have liberal views but in fact is merely a conventional snob who believes in the importance of "birth" and the necessity of marrying one's social equals or "betters." The evidence was there to be seen, however, for Miss Crawley would call Becky her social equal in one breath and in the next ask her to put some coals on the fire or to alter a dress—so that we may conclude that Becky, like most of the inhabitants of Vanity Fair, saw only what she wanted to see. When the identity of Becky's husband is revealed, the responses of Miss Crawley and Sir Pitt contrast remarkably with the images of them that we received in number 3. There we learned how her wealth gave her "dignity" (9) in the eyes especially of her relatives, and we saw the full-page illustration, *Miss Crawley's affectionate relatives*, depicting her sitting comfortably in a chair enjoying being attended by four toadying figures. Here in number 5, however, she becomes hysterical at receiving the news, wildly (but with considerable validity) accuses Mrs. Bute of plotting against Rawdon, and finally faints upon hearing Mrs. Bute's malicious revelations, which are both true and false. The comedy is dark, but still amusing.

In the case of Sir Pitt, however, the limits of comedy seem to be reached, for the person described in number 3 as a man of "rank, and honours and power," "a dignitary of the land" (9), who responds in number 5 to the news of Rawdon's marriage is a "frenzied old man, wild with hatred and insane with baffled desire" (16). On returning to Queen's Crawley, where he formerly ruled everyone, he bursts "like a madman" into Becky's room and scatters her possessions everywhere. The narrator then completes this extraordinary image of disorder: "Miss Horrocks, the butler's daughter, took some of [the clothes]. The children dressed themselves and acted plays in the others. It was but a few days after the poor mother had gone to her lonely burying-place; and was laid, unwept and disregarded, in a vault full of strangers." The narrative representation of the chaos that Becky causes, which will be repeated elsewhere, leads to a requiem for the former Rose Dawson and a reminder that as inhabitants of Vanity Fair we all live not only in a world of time, but also essentially in darkness.

Another image of dispersal follows with the bankruptcy of Sedley and the auctioning of his household effects. The return of Becky to London in the previous number had begun to bring the novel's two plots together, as she reestablished her association with Amelia and George, promptly putting him down with the same haughty gesture that Miss Pinkerton had unsuccessfully tried to use against her. Here in chapter 17 the dispersal attracts her, prompts her amusement, and gives her the opportunity to buy Jos's portrait—which will figure significantly in the final double number, while Dobbin, who does not derive amusement from the unpleasant auction, successfully outbids her attempts to buy Amelia's piano—which will also later serve importantly in the narrative.

The contrast of fortunes in number 4 between George and Old Sedley here in number 5 finds a parallel in the bankruptcy that was there foreshadowed, and in the contrast between the Sedley family's fortunes and those of Becky and Rawdon, who succesfully live upon credit. Similarly, Osborne's earlier brutal threats to break off George's marriage to Amelia are here actually carried out. Finally, of course, the promise at the end of number 3 that Becky would be a match for father and son, and her revelation at the end of number 4 to Sir Pitt that she was already married, are succeeded here at the end of number 5 by Dobbin's success in persuading George to marry Amelia.

A final link between numbers 3, 4, and 5 is established by three passages of narrative commentary, at the end of chapters 8, 12, and 15. In the former, the narrator asks us to perceive the distinction between himself and the characters in the narrative so that he can successfully carry out the purpose of his satirical comedy: "to combat and expose" (8) folly so that we may achieve an understanding not only of folly, but of wisdom and goodness. Then, in Chapter 12, he makes a distinction between two kinds of human behavior: one, like Becky's, motivated by "Shift, Self, and Poverty" (12) and emblemized by the orange blossoms of mercenary marriages; the other, like Amelia's, motivated by "idolatry and silly romantic ideas."

Both are folly, but seeing the cold, calculating attempt to use marriage as an instrument for providing wealth and physical comforts for one's self can help us to understand the superiority of Amelia's warmhearted feelings for George, no matter how excessive they are. Her feelings are those of "devotion" for another person, not for her-self—a devotion, moreover, that is "blind" not only because it distorts George but also because it is uncalculating. At this particular moment, therefore, the narrator rejects a role of exposure, like that of Iachimo, for a quietly illuminating one, like that of Moonshine, in order to reveal the "faith and beauty and innocence" of Amelia's love, in con-trast to the "Faithless, Hopeless, Charityless" (8) Beckys and Crawleys of the world.

The corresponding passage of narrative commentary in number 5 refers explicitly to this passage as the narrator now looks at Becky: "If, a few pages back, the present writer claimed the privilege of peep-ing into Miss Amelia Sedley's bed-room, and understanding with the omniscience of the novelist all the gentle pains and passions which were tossing upon that innocent pillow, why should he not declare himself to be Rebecca's confidante too, master of her secrets, and seal-keeper of that young woman's conscience?" (15). Here the narrative mode becomes that of exposure, as we learn of Becky's calculations regarding Miss Crawley's acceptance of the marriage.

In short, by recalling to us the passage of commentary in the pre-vious installment, which is linked to the corresponding passage in chapter 8, the narrator shows how the comic purpose enunciated there becomes a mode of illumination in chapter 12 and one of exposure in chapter 15. A "well regulated mind" (12), in his ironic phrase, arranges mercenary, orange blossom marriages. His ironic "fear [that] poor Emmy had not a well regulated mind" is therefore a form of praise. When a similar phrase occurs in chapter 15, the narrator of course applies it to Becky and to those like her who devote themselves to selfish calculation and therefore cannot understand that the oppor-tunity to marry Sir Pitt is the opposite of "a piece of marvellous good fortune" (15). The failure of her calculations to consider the possibility of Lady Crawley's death, moreover, strongly suggests the improbability of her calculations regarding Miss Crawley and reminds us how human calculation is inevitably circumscribed by the incalculable.

Numbers 6 and 7 concern themselves largely with the maneuverings of Mrs. Bute, Becky, Old Osborne, and, contrastingly, Dobbin. While Mrs. Bute takes control of Miss Crawley and her household and seeks to alienate Miss Crawley from Becky and Rawdon with vicious reports of them, Dobbin becomes George's diplomatic representative in London and seeks to gain acceptance for the marriage of George and Amelia by detailing their virtues to George's sister. Like Becky in the previous installment, Mrs. Bute wishes she had a more intelligent husband to assist her in her schemes. In fact, she manages too well, and though she succeeds in blackening the characers of Becky and Rawdon, she creates in her victim, Miss Crawley "a great hatred and secret terror of her victimiser" (19). Just as the children in number 7 in archetypal fashion "pay their court" (23) to the one with the penny, so do the adults in number 6. The failure of Becky and Rawdon to appeal successfully to Miss Crawley in the park, however, is simply the first of several failures in these two numbers of schemes to control or placate the adults who have the money: Miss Crawley and Old Osborne.

The only successful arranger is Dobbin, who persuades George in number 6 to marry Amelia, but who of course cannot, in the corresponding portion of number 7, make Old Osborne accept it. Ironically, Old Osborne's violent rage is paired with Old Sedley's grim smile "of something like satisfaction" (20) at the idea that Old Osborne would suffer such a blow—a smile that in turn is partly reflected in the "strange look" (24) that passes over Old Osborne's face as he says, after having signed a new will disinheriting George, "And now . . . my mind will be easy." In spite of their pretenses, however, both men have been "visibly shattered."

The failure of Old Osborne's attempt in number 6 to force his son to marry Miss Swartz, leads in number 7 to the father's only remaining power, which is expressed in a letter written by his lawyer to George and telling him that, aside from being paid his mother's bequest, he will receive no more money. Even as Old Osborne pretends that he can deny George's existence as a member of his family, George is never more his father's son than in his response to the letter, for his father had said in number 6 that he would tolerate no "dam sentimental nonsense" (21) about a marriage to Amelia, and now in number 7 George says he is a beggar, "and all in consequence of my d—d sentimentality" (25). Whereas George had prudently collected money from Mr. Chopper before quarreling with his father, now in Brighton it is being collected from him by Rawdon.

Previously, George's vanity had been greatly flattered by Amelia's humble gratitude for his love. Consequently, in arguing with his father he had projected himself as a man of honor who had to respect the terms of his engagement. Partly out of angry discomfort at his father's challenge to this image of himself, therefore, he sets the wedding date: "'I'll marry her to-morrow,' he said with an oath" (21). After the marriage his hypocritical self-delusion continues, notably when, upon receiving the news of being disinherited by his father, he projects the image of himself as a thoughtful husband who cannot bear Amelia's being deprived of her rightful "comforts and station in society" (25), whereas the real reason for his anxiety, as he has just told Dobbin, is the threat to his *own* position: "How the deuce am I to keep up my position in the world? . . . I *must* have my comforts."

When Mrs. Bute takes her patient, Miss Crawley, to the resort of Brighton, Becky and Rawdon of course follow after them and in Brighton meet George, Amelia, Jos, and the visiting Dobbin. The conclusion of number 6, therefore, reestablishes this series of relationships and ends with the news of the army's being ordered to Belgium. The conclusion of number 7, following two initial chapters of restrospective narration, also takes place in Brighton as the main characters prepare to leave for Belgium and as Becky and Rawdon make a final assault upon Miss Crawley, following the unexpected overthrow of Mrs. Bute's control. Becky wins over Miss Briggs easily enough, but fails with the letter to Miss Crawley that she dictates to Rawdon precisely because of what she brings from her background: the need to spell correctly and to write grammatically.

Here is the final failure of purposeful individuals in these two installments to control other people. Miss Crawley unhappily knows that her relatives want her dead and are hankering for her money, but it she who finally triumphs, being freed from Mrs. Bute and freeing herself from Becky and Rawdon by setting the bait of money in London. Only Becky can successfully deal with the news of Miss Crawley's deception, however, so *she* has the final laugh: "Though it told against themselves, the joke was too good, and Becky burst out laughing at Rawdon's discomfiture" (25).

An especially notable series of parallels and contrasts character-izes the movement toward Brussels and Waterloo in numbers 8 and 9, showing us that a full understanding of paired serial installments requires that we recall the past number while reading the present one. Thus we not only see the timidity and inexperience of the newly mar-ried Amelia in number 8, but we perceive her shortcomings more fully when we see the practical and effective as well as affectionate minis-trations of Mrs. O'Dowd in number 9, as she makes preparations for her husband's departure for battle. So, too, as we see the happiness that marriage causes Rawdon to feel in number 9 and recall the melan-choly effect of marriage upon Amelia in number 8, we understand each response better because of the additional context that the unfold-ing serial has provided.

All the little pleasures of his previous life seem insipid compared to the pleasures of having Becky live with him and entertain him, as a result of which "he loved and worshipped her with all his faculties of regard and admiration" (30). This language contains its own qualifica-tions, of course, because we know and Becky repeatedly comments on his limited capacities, but the narrative language that characterizes Amelia's melancholy had already emphasized the inappropriateness and inevitable disillusionment of any worship other than religious devotion. Her disappointment arises from her gradually increasing awareness of the difference between the real George and "that superb young hero whom she had worshipped" (26). Inevitably, therefore, this disillusioning experience causes her "to be looking sadly and vaguely back." Her experience in fact embodies the quintessential folly of seeking happiness in Vanity Fair: "always to be pining for some-thing which, when obtained, brought doubt and sadness rather than pleasure: here was the lot of our poor little creature, and harmless lost wanderer in the great struggling crowds of Vanity Fair."

Amelia, therefore, though her awareness is quite limited, has a better understanding of the folly of human desire than does Rawdon or, especially, George, who is incapable of reflective awareness and who engages in almost nothing *but* the pursuit of pleasure. Hence, as we recall how he arrogantly collected his mother's bequest and began his ostentatious dispersal of it, we can appreciate more fully the touchingly comical scene in which dense Rawdon notes down, "in his big school-boy handwriting, the various items of his portable property which might be sold for his widow's advantage" (30)—affectionately thinking of her welfare, but being utterly numb to the implications of his possessing duelling pistols "(same which I shot Captain Marker)," for example. Becky, characteristically, feels nothing after his departure except satisfaction at her calculation of her possessions and estimation of her financial prospects.

As George rejoins his regiment in Chatham, accompanied by Amelia and Jos, Mrs. O'Dowd emerges into prominence, contrasting both with Amelia and Becky, especially in her good-natured, domineering manner. In the following number, as the battle with Napoleon approaches, Dobbin—not George—asks Jos to care for Amelia and take her back to England in case of a defeat. Unlike Mrs. O'Dowd or Becky, Amelia is at her most helpless in parting from her husband, who is happy to leave her, unlike the emotionally moved Rawdon or the even-tempered Major O'Dowd. Two early morning military departures then help time the narrative, as the transports load their cargoes for Belgium at the end of chapter 27 and as the regiment marches off to battle at the end of chapter 30.

The presence of Jos comically extends the contrast between the military and domestic figures. Seeing himself as a quasimilitary counterpart of the army officers, he agrees to escort Amelia and Mrs. O'Dowd to Belgium in chapter 28, and subsequently finds himself "in command of the little colony at Brussels" (31). Belgium proves to be a country devoted to commerce and survival, motives epitomized in the figure of Jos's rapacious servant, Isidor, whose servile flattery of "My lord" (28) Sedley amusingly contrasts with his later, open acknowledgment, amid rumors of a French victory, that he is a "partisan of Napoleon" (31). Those unsettling rumors also contrast with the previous confidence of the English travelers who thronged Brussels and enjoyed its pleasures. Becky's triumphant arrival in Brussels amid the entourage of General Tufto at the end of chapter 28 also contrasts with her later flattery of Jos in order to secure a place in his carriage, should retreat become necessary, while Amelia's sadness at Becky's arrival has grown into overt hostility by the end of chapter 31.

The sadness ensues from the attention George has paid to Becky in Brighton, of course, while the hostility follows from his infatuation with her in Brussels—which we see in the final chapter of number 8. Both it and the ending of number 9 dramatize an unusual amount of deception and self-deception, even for Vanity Fair. In the former, Becky acts to entice General Tufto in his box at the opera and then uses George to provoke the General's jealousy, while George imagines himself to be "a woman-killer and destined to conquer" (29). Their farcical contrasts in chapter 32 are Regulus Van Cutsum, who imagines himself to be a warrior, and the terrified Jos, who imagines that he will be mistaken for one.

The night of the ball on the eve of Waterloo, however, best epitomizes the triumph of deception and self-deception, as Becky achieves her greatest social success to date (which will last for one evening), insults Amelia, and responds to the sight of George's note with a knowing but noncommital look, which he overeagerly interprets, and in turn goes off, gambles frantically, wins, and exultantly rushes off to prepare for war. Becky also dominates in the amusingly contrasting chapter 32, this time as she triumphs over Lord and Lady Bareacres (the name itself expressing pretense), rejecting their note of entreaty and sneeringly laughing in the face of the Countess, before offering her horses to the frantic Jos, who pays an immense sum for them, and prepares to flee the city.

Finally, however, at the end of both serial installments, military reality asserts itself. With the news that the army will march in three hours, George returns to his quarters, makes preparations to leave, feels a momentary regret for his behavior toward Amelia, and takes leave of her. In chapter 32, Jos hears the news of the Allied victory at Quatre Bras and is calmed for a time, until he hears the cannon of Waterloo roar and instantly flees, abandoning Amelia. The numbers end with *Vanity Fair*'s most startling serial contrasts: dawn and the awakening of Brussels to the sound of bugle, drums, and pipes in number 8, and night, as "darkness came down on the field and city, and Amelia was praying for George, who was lying on his face, dead, with a bullet through his heart" (32) in number 9.

The next two serial installments take us from the Continent back to England—beginning in chapter 33 as Miss Crawley's relatives, especially Pitt, continue their attempts to cultivate her approval and secure her money, and in chapter 36 as Becky manages to settle with Rawdon's creditors, thereby making possible a return to London. Pitt and Becky are therefore the dominating figures. In number 10 she uses Rawdon's military promotion and their ensuing residence in Paris as pretexts for a series of ingratiating letters to Miss Crawley, but the efforts, as we can imagine, inevitably fail to overcome the old lady's hostility. In number 11 their continuing monetary difficulties force Rawdon to quit the Guards and sell out of the army, and though Becky's ability to charm other people succeeds in Parisian society, she recognizes that she and Rawdon must make their future in London, and therefore negotiates their safe return.

Pitt uses tactics similar to those formerly used by Becky, as he cultivates Miss Briggs and brings a gentle, attractive young lady—in this case not Amelia but her counterpart, Lady Jane—to see Miss Crawley. The comedy here arises not only from Pitt's shrewd, hypocritical maneuvers, but also from the contrast between himself and Becky on the one hand, and Lady Jane on the other, for Lady Jane ingratiates herself with Miss Crawley not with calculation but naturally, with "artless sweetness and friendship" (34). Her naturalness also contrasts with that of James Crawley, whose attempt to win Miss Crawley's favor, proves to be only a difficulty easily overcome by Pitt and by James's own ineptitude. In the corresponding portion of number 11 Becky and Rawdon succeed in establishing themselves in London, but Becky cannot overcome the female opposition that she meets and finds herself rejected by good society.

Her contrasting success in Paris had been detailed in chapter 34, but even there her triumphs were limited, for her very giving birth to a son and *heir* immediately causes Miss Crawley to take decisive countermeasures. In order to produce an heir who would take precedence over Rawdon's son, she insists on Pitt's marriage to Lady Jane and changes her will to give the bulk of her fortune to Pitt while Becky and Rawdon are trying to live on nothing a year. In chapter 34 the narrator had spoken of Miss Crawley's impending death; in chapter 37 that event takes place, prompting contrasting reactions from Pitt's relatives: estranging abuse from Bute, and a "frank, manly, good-humoured letter" (37) from Rawdon—another dictation of Becky's, who wants Lady Jane to be her sponsor in London society. Having achieved his monetary goal, however, Pitt finds himself dominated by "his aunt on one side, and . . . his mother-in-law on the other" (34), while in number 11 the submissive male is Rawdon, who is no longer "Colonel Crawley," but "Mrs. Crawley's husband" (37).

The final chapters of numbers 10 and 11 return us to the Osbornes and Sedleys, first as we see the effects of George's death on Amelia and on Old Osborne. Rigid and impervious as ever, the latter cannot come to terms with the death and with his responsibilities, except to order an ostentatious monument for his son, while she collapses into a delirium that is succeeded by blank depression. The pitiable sight of Amelia produces in him only an enraged rejection of her and of her unborn child. The parallel figure in the ensuing serial installment is Old Sedley, who, full of ostentatious talk and empty financial schemes, is in truth a "feeble and stricken old man" (38), pathetically "shattered and stranded." His daughter seems to recover with the birth of young George in chapter 35, but we see there and again in chapter 38 that the recovery is only partial. As she did when George was alive, so too she magnifies him in death, turning the days of her marriage and widowhood into occasions for ritual worship as of a departed saint. Finally, the two numbers end on the same note: the continuance of Dobbin's devotion and the continuance of Amelia's refusal to allow room for anyone in her life except young George.

Changes of scene to Queen's Crawley and India mark the opening of numbers 12 and 13, which begin with narratives of attempted marriages and threatening marriages. Mrs. Bute grimly accepts her failure to secure for her husband a large portion of Miss Crawley's fortune, but publicly she pretends that the inheritance has been sizable and energetically pursues her major remaining objective: to marry her unattractive daughters. Pitt, on the other hand, is horrified to see that his doddering old father has apparently become even more intimately involved with Miss Horrocks, his butler's daughter; accordingly, Pitt trembles daily lest she become his father's third wife. Miss Horrocks ("Ribbons") in turn imagines that she will actually become Lady Crawley and begins to pretend that she is a fine lady—to the immense amusement of Sir Pitt, who apparently has no intention of making another low and in this case unprofitable marriage, as we can infer from his gift of family pearls to Lady Jane and his accompanying remark: "never gave 'em the ironmonger's daughter" (39).

Moving to India, we see a domineering woman who nevertheless contrasts with Mrs. Bute in Lady O'Dowd, who is "a tyrant over her Michael: a dragon amongst all the ladies of the regiment: a mother to all the young men" (43). She too has a matchmaking purpose, however: to marry her sister Glorvina to Dobbin. Because Glorvina has been unsuccessfully trying for years to catch a man, she actively sets about trying to attract Dobbin, deluding herself into thinking that she can overcome his indifference toward her. He, also wanting what he cannot have, thinks obsessively about Amelia, and, upon receiving news that Amelia is planning to marry, immediately sets off in an absurd attempt to prevent her marriage.

Following the stroke suffered by his father, Pitt assumes control of Queen's Crawley and, upon succeeding to the title of baronet, sends another in the series of carefully studied letters that are to be found throughout the narrative—this one *to* Becky instead of *from* her. In this case, however, the letter inviting her to the funeral of old Sir Pitt, is a means of asserting control over his mother-in-law rather than an attempt to deceive its recipient. We then observe lateral *developments* between serial installments when we see that as a result of officially joining the family and ingratiating herself in chapter 40 with the new Sir Pitt, Becky in chapter 44 comes to be in charge of renovating his London town house in Great Gaunt Street.

After recalling his letter of invitation to her, we see a further development in the latter chapter, as he actually gives her a check for young Rawdon. Similarly, we recall her delight in receiving the letter and, in noticing her much more restrained response to the gift, we understand how more precarious her financial situation has become, and how the little gift represents her failure to secure a larger sum from Sir Pitt for Rawdon and herself. A more sinister development occurs as a result of her securing Miss Briggs to be "guardian of her innocence and reputation" (40), for by using Miss Briggs as a "house-dog" to free herself from the necessity of Rawdon's presence, she causes her servants and her landlord to "believe . . . her to be guilty" (44) of using that freedom to establish a sexual relationship with Lord Steyne.

The sequence of lateral developments continues with the two visits of Becky and Rawdon to Queen's Crawley. During the former, Becky has considerable success in charming Sir Pitt and Lady Jane, especially in the absence of young Rawdon, but her success with Lady Jane is more limited during the second visit, precisely because young Rawdon, whom she has grown to dislike, blurts out some rather chilling information about her treatment of him. At the end of the first visit, Becky's ability to conciliate the baronet and his wife helps prompt Lady Jane's gift of a bank note for young Rawdon, Sir Pitt's promise to pay for the boy's schooling, and the wish for a London reunion. At the end of the second visit, her even greater success with Sir Pitt prompts him actually to give Rawdon £100, but she and Lady Jane part "with some alacrity" (45) and keep apart in London. As the relationship beteeen Becky and Sir Pitt continues to develop, and as he comes to visit Becky daily, the closeness among Rawdon and his son and Lady Jane also increases, as they find a second home with her.

As with the two previous installments, numbers 12 and 13 end with a narrative return to the Osbornes and Sedleys, in this case as the narrator overtly calls attention to a series of contrasts between the two households. Continuing to prosper economically, but feeling great unhappiness and growing more violent, Old Osborne tyranizes over everyone around him, while feeble Old Sedley, secretly engaged in his impossible speculations, succeeds only in undermining his impoverished family's security. Maria Osborne escapes into a mercenary marriage with her father's approval, and she soon develops a snobbish coldness toward him, leaving him for company only her sister Jane, whom he forces to remain single and bullies into dejected submission so that she can keep house for him. Her miserable life is the one constant in the two serial installments, causing the narrator to evoke her "awful existence" (42) in number 12, and then to recall that life as "a lonely, miserable, persecuted old maid" (46) in number 13.

The final development occurring across the numbers concerns the relationships among Jane, young George, and Old Osborne. At the end of chapter 42 she sees young George for the first time, gives him her watch and gold chain, and tells her father, who flushes and trembles at the news. In chapter 46 the narrator recalls that event, as Old Osborne replaces her watch and chain and then goes himself to see young George, trembling at the sight of the boy. As a result, he offers to take young George into his house, to make him his heir, and to provide income for Amelia. The chapter and number end as Amelia, learning the results of her father's failed speculations, concludes that Old Osborne's offer indeed represents her son's future.

Numbers 14, 15, and 16 all begin by focusing on Lord Steyne and Becky, the middle number being entirely devoted to them, while the others numbers end by returning to Amelia and young George. Chapter 47, "Gaunt House," is a remarkable evocation of secret, "back-door" activities, conspiratorial, luxurious, and sexual, as well as of a family divided against itself and stricken with madness and the threat of madness. Having been invited to Gaunt House, Becky finds that "some of the very greatest and tallest doors in the metropolis were speedily opened to her" (51). Her greatest triumph, however, occurs at Gaunt House itself, where she sparkles in the illusionistic setting of a charade theater, and where her charade roles of Clytemnestra and Philomela evoke illicit love and murderously divided families. The precariousness of her triumphs then appears at the beginning of number 16 where, in Sir Pitt's house in Great Gaunt Street, the arrival of a newspaper giving an account of "Festivities at Gaunt House" (54) is soon succeeded by the arrival of a disheveled Rawdon, who tells Sir Pitt of the end of his marriage to Becky, and of the sinister relationship between her and Steyne.

With Becky's triumphant presentation at court in number 14, she momentarily achieves her "aim in life": "to be, and to be thought, a respectable woman" (48). With her success in getting £1,125 from Steyne, on the pretext that she owes it to Miss Briggs, she manages to keep herself financially afloat, but also puts aside £1,000 in what will be an unsuccessful attempt to provide for her future. In the parallel chapter of number 15, Steyne discovers her deception, but succeeds in removing Miss Briggs as well as young Rawdon from Becky's household. In the parallel chaper of number 16, the anarchy beneath the surface of Becky's life emerges personally in her, comically in the rebellion of her household servants, and grimly in the bankruptcy of Raggles and in the demoralized acceptance by Rawdon of his fatal appointment. Becky finally rallies from her "state of stupor and confusion" (55), but the game is over: following the exposure in Curzon Street that occurs at the end of number 15, Rawdon has the £1,000 note returned to Steyne and goes off to Coventry Island, while Steyne leaves for the Continent.

Becky's limited success had continued in number 14 as Steyne arranged for her invitation to Gaunt House, but there she found herself rejected by all the women except Lady Steyne, who pitied her. The contrasting analogue in number 15 is Rawdon's finding himself a prisoner in a bailiff's house, writing unsuccessfully to Becky, having her reject his plea, and then finding assistance when Lady Jane pities him and comes to release him. With the collapse of Becky's schemes and the departure of Rawdon, the narrative turns in number 16 to young George, who has become fully established in the home of Old Osborne and enjoys all kinds of comforts and luxuries, having his letters delivered upon a silver tray, as we see in the illustration, *Georgy a Gentleman* (56), and being toadied to by everyone around him, including his grandfather and his schoolmaster.

These developments follow, of course, from the ending of number 14, where Amelia, responding to the financial irresponsibility of her father, the hysterical attacks of her mother, and the promptings of her own sense of unworthiness, decides to give him up into the care of Old Osborne—a decision to which young George responds with delight at the prospect of beginning such an opulent life. Number 15 concludes, as we have seen, with the contrasting picture of the ending of a way of life—Becky's and Rawdon's in Curzon Street, which collapses as Rawdon returns home to find Becky and Steyne in a compromising situation—while the conclusion of number 16 shows us Amelia bearing up under the behavior of her complaining mother and dottering father, but also facing the beginning of a new mode of life as Jos and Dobbin return from India.

Numbers 17 and 18 both begin with passages of narrative commentary, that in number 17 reflecting upon the "lottery of life" (57) that gives individuals like Old Osborne and Old Sedley such different fates, and that in the following installment meditating upon the second-floor arch and concluding with an awareness of death as our common fate. In chapter 57 Old Osborne triumphs in the fact that Old Sedley's poverty forces him to accept his enemy's money but the shortly ensuing death of Mrs. Sedley points ahead to what follows in chapter 61: the death of both men. While living in "long, ignoble bondage" in Clapham, Amelia leads a life of "solitary imprisonment" (57) from which she is rescued more by the reappearance of Dobbin and Jos than by the inheritance she later receives from Old Osborne, which, although it gives her financial independence, also subjects her to a society "too cruelly genteel" (61) for her.

The disembarkation of Dobbin and Jos in England is succeeded in number 18 by their embarkation for the Continent in the company of Amelia and young George. If Dobbin had made a point of dressing in his best civilian clothes to see Amelia in chapter 58, Jos outdoes him in Pumpernickel in the splendor of "his court dress" (62). Indeed, his pomposity finds a perfect arena in the duchy. The relationship between Dobbin and Amelia, however, receives the chief emphasis in the two installments. Whether they are quite reticent, as we see at their moment of reunion, when both remain "speechless" (58), or whether they talk "with some spirit" (59), as in their exchange when the revelation about her treasured piano finally causes him to speak, her frightened unwillingness to emerge from her widowhood produces a remarkably one-sided resolution: "And so William was at liberty to look and long."

In Germany, however, their relationship finally shows signs of change as Amelia becomes unusually happy and as her inner capacities begin to develop—especially under the influence of the operas of Mozart and Cimarosa: "A new world of love and beauty broke upon her when she was introduced to those divine compositions" (62). Being educated by this experience and by close, extended association with Dobbin in the presence of her son, who likes the Major, she seems to be developing more knowledgeable and mature capacities. Later, this period will apparently come to seem to them "the happiest time of both their lives," but of course their marriage does not grow naturally and inevitably out of this association; instead, there has to be a crisis, as we see toward the novel's end.

The final chapter of number 17 shows us how "Good fortune now begins to smile upon Amelia" (60), as Jos establishes a house in London, where she lives comfortably, attended by a maid and a page, with a visiting book and with a carriage at her disposal. The final chapter of Number 18 reintroduces her lifelong contrast, Becky, alone, in a somewhat soiled dress, losing her wagers at roulette. One constant in both numbers, however, is Jos, leading "a life of dignified otiosity." In the former he goes to court, as Becky had done, accompanied by Dobbin in a shabby old uniform reminiscent of Rawdon's, while Amelia jokes about the lack of family diamonds, rather than wearing diamonds surreptitiously given to her, like those given to Becky by Steyne and Sir Pitt. In the latter, we receive hints about how a previous pattern is about to be reenacted as Jos, in his Court suit, comes to the gambling room and meets Becky, who once again begins to play her seductive games upon him.

The four chapters of the final double installment complete this series of contrasting actions and relationships. Chapter 64 gives us a retrospective account of Becky's life since the catastrophe in Curzon Street. After initially feeling "a kind of despair" (64) that causes her to neglect her person and even her reputation, she rallies and determinedly seeks to reestablish herself and her respectability, loving society as she does, but is repeatedly rejected, forced to change her places of residence and made to lead the vagabond life that eventually brings her to Pumpernickel. In chapter 66 she adroitly embroiders upon these misfortunes to play upon Amelia's sympathies, giving what the narrator ironically calls "a full and complete version of her private history" (66). Amelia, being a born victim, pities Becky and takes her into her house in spite of Dobbin's urging that she reject Becky, thereby creating the crisis in their relationship that causes Dobbin to break off and leave Pumpernickel.

Having reestablished contact with Jos and given him in Chapter 65 an affecting history of her difficulties, Becky finds in him a sympathetic hearer who becomes her means of touching Amelia's sensibilities. Although Amelia resists part of the story, she responds in a puppetlike manner, instantly abandoning her earlier skepticism, when Jos relates Becky's fictional melodramatic account of being separated from her son. The chapter ends as she rushes over to Becky's hotel and embraces her, while Dobbin disapprovingly looks on. The final contrasts occur in chapter 67, as Becky extends her ingratiating influence over the household, as she has often done elsewhere, making Jos "her sworn slave and frantic admirer" (67), and praising Dobbin to Amelia. Without Dobbin, Amelia is unprotected, as the presence of Becky's sleazy male friends emphasizes. Needing his protection, therefore, she finally emerges from her enclosed, rigidly maintained little world of widowhood and sends him the letter of capitulation, causing him to return to her. The conclusive embrace in this chapter, therefore, has Amelia finally bestow it upon an appropriate person, Dobbin, who ends his years as an observer, finally becoming a participant.

Looking at *Vanity Fair* from a more distant perspective, we see that this serially composed narrative organizes itself not only in terms of chapters and individual serial numbers but also in terms of nine larger groupings. The first begins with Becky's and Amelia's departure from Chiswick Mall and with the opening of Becky's campaign against Jos (number 1), ending with her failure to capture him and her subsequent departure from London for Queen's Crawley (number 2). The second large phase of the narrative begins as she ingratiates herself at Queen's Crawley, especially with Sir Pitt (number 3), then continues with Amelia's romantic difficulties and with Becky's marriage to Sir Pitt's son (number 4), and concludes with Sedley's bankruptcy and George's proposal to Amelia (number 5). Here are several climaxes:

first with the revelation that Becky is already married, second with the discovery of her husband's identity, and finally with George's proposal to Amelia. The third phase concerns itself with unsuccessful efforts to conciliate the two people toward whom the monetary expectations of Rawdon and George are directed: Miss Crawley and Old Osborne (numbers 6 and 7). Phase four (numbers 8 and 9) then carries us toward Waterloo, where Amelia loses the husband she had gained at the end of phase two. Waterloo, indeed, represents the most memorable climax of the narrative, except for the novel's ending.

The remaining five-ninths of the narrative begins with Pitt's success in becoming Miss Crawley's heir, with Dobbin's departure for India after his continued failure to make himself a part of Amelia's life, and with Becky's and Rawdon's establishing themselves in Curzon Street, London (numbers 10 and 11). Phase six (numbers 12 and 13) concerns itself with the aftermath of Old Sir Pitt's death, as Becky conciliates his son and flatters his social and political ambitions, and with Old Osborne, who relents toward young George and prepares to take him into his house. In the central phase of the remaining five-ninths of the narrative, phase seven, we find another group of three closely related numbers (14, 15, and 16), which take us from the dubious splendors of Gaunt House to the bankruptcy of Raggles, and to the return of Dobbin from India. The climax here comes at the end of the middle number, as Becky and Steyne are discovered by Rawdon and as the marriage revealed at the end of the middle number of phase two is now permanently disrupted.

The narrative's two final phases therefore trace Amelia's success in being able to accept a second husband. Phase eight (numbers 17 and 18) narrates the deaths of the remaining members of the older generation, Old Sedley and his wife, and Old Osborne, the financial independence of Amelia, her growing intimacy with Dobbin, and the reappearance of Becky. Finally, in phase nine (the final double number, numbers 19 and 20), we see the marriage that counterbalances Amelia's loss of George at the end of phase four. All that remains is for Becky, who initiated the long pattern of rejections in chapter 1, to be rejected in turn by Dobbin and Amelia at the end of the narrative.

6

The Narrator

MOMENTARY OMNISCIENCE

Aside from narrators who tell their own story, like Jane Eyre, the narrator of *Vanity Fair* is perhaps the most prominent narrator in nineteenth-century fiction. Indeed, some readers think he is the most important personage in *Vanity Fair*. Again, aside from autobiographical narrators, he is perhaps the one who most immediately and constantly shapes our ongoing awareness of the implications of the narrative. The most omnipresent and form-changing of narrators, he is a protean figure, mirroring the archetypal configurations of human society in all their ambiguity as well as their clarity. The metamorphoses of the narrator, therefore, reflect his belief that one cannot see and understand the ambiguity of human life from a single, stable point of view.

Even his role of manager of the performance, though of major importance, is not all-encompassing. His first definition of his role is pictorial, for in the cover illustration of each serial installment he presents himself as a jester standing on top of a barrel addressing an audience of fools. Later, at the end of chapter 9, he draws himself as a solitary, melancholy jester (with the face of Thackeray) holding a grinning mask. Still later, as the narrative is approaching its end, in a new title page he presents himself again as a solitary jester, this time leaning against a box of puppets, with a lath sword at his side, staring into a cracked mirror while sitting on a stage that extends into the world offstage. At about this same time he writes "Before the Curtain," where he identifies himself as manager of the performance.

As a narrator he is overtly inconsistent. After stating that because Amelia "is not a heroine, there is no need to describe her person" (1), he goes on to do just that, although with some comically qualifying language, including the characterization of her as a "silly thing" for her readiness to cry. Yet in the very next chapter he calls her "the heroine of this work . . . whom we have selected for the very reason that she was the best-natured of all" (2). This narrative inconsistency, therefore, tells us that Amelia is *both* a heroine, because of her good nature, and not a heroine, because of her weakness. The running heads at the top of every other page of the serial installments and the title page for the single volume of 1848 proclaim that this is "A Novel without a Hero," as indeed it is. Yet it also has a hero of sorts in Dobbin, because of his good nature. The narrator ironically calls Jos a "hero" (30), which he emphatically is not, in any sense of the term, but the narrator also ironically calls Becky "a heroine" (30)—which she both is, because of her vitality and strength, and is not, because of her amorality and "her hostility to her kind" (2).

Another aspect of the narrator's meaningful inconsistency appears in his contradictory statements about his knowledge—at one moment claiming omniscience, and at another acknowledging that he has only limited awareness. As we begin to listen to the narrator of *Vanity Fair,* we notice that he is mediating to us what he calls "this little world of history" (1), *history* being a word originating from classical Greek, where it means "knowledge" or "knowing." We may notice also that the narrator's initial use of the first person occurs in the same sentence, where he uses it to unite himself with us, and to speak with probability, not certainty: "It is probable that we shall not hear of

[Jemima] again from this moment to the end of time, and that when the great filligree iron gates are closed upon her, she and her awful sister will never issue therefrom into this little world of history." That sentence joins "I" and "you" into "we," but it also implies that in some sense narrator and reader both inhabit the world of the narrative—or, in other words, that there is no sharp demarcation between fiction and what we sometimes, and perhaps too confidently, call reality. He is quite aware of the distinction, but, as elsewhere, he emphasizes the connection between "life and . . . novels" (1) when he asks: "Are not there little chapters in every body's life . . . ?" (6).

The narrator defines himself as a man writing to human beings, who has lived some years among them, and who can therefore imagine reactions to different portions of his narrative. Therefore, after telling us of the schoolgirls' feelings at the prospect of Amelia's departure from Miss Pinkerton's, the narrator says: "All which details, I have no doubt, JONES who reads this book at his club, will pronounce to be excessively foolish trivial twaddling and ultrasentimental. Yes, I can see Jones at this minute"—the minute he is writing the yet unprinted words that the symbolic Jones will read. Because Jones is symbolic—a figure representing various limited human beings—and because Jones's reaction is in the future, the narrator, by virtue of his own experience and imagination, is claiming representative knowledge and foreknowledge.

When the narrator tells us, in an aside, that "novelists have the privilege of knowing every thing" (3), he is referring to his knowledge that Joseph Sedley "thought a great deal about the girl up stairs"—Becky Sharp, whom Jos has just met and with whom he has had lunch. This claim of omniscience is therefore partly comical because it refers to what anyone with informed knowledge and imagination could infer. The same can be said of his later claims to know "everything" (33, 36).

When he refers to the cover illustration and calls himself a moralist who wears "the very same long-eared livery" (8) as the members of his congregation, and who feels "bound to speak the truth as far as one knows it," one understands that his claims to know everything can be understood in terms of the oxymoron, *momentary omniscience.* Like Jones and the other members of his audience, he is both in and out of the novel and cannot *rest* in any claim of omniscience. As he had already said early in the second serial installment, again addressing members of his audience directly, "how much do you and I know of each other, of our children, of our fathers, of our neighbour . . . ?" (5).

As Dobbin rises up to stop Cuff from beating George, the narrator informs us, "I can't tell what his motive was"—but he immmediately goes on to speculate: "Perhaps Dobbin's foolish soul revolted against that exercise of tyranny: or perhaps he had a hankering feeling of revenge in his mind and longed to measure himself against that splendid bully and tyrant." In short, the narrator refuses to offer a simple explanation or to be omniscient; instead he gives *us* the responsibility of making a knowledgeable inference. Similarly, when Pitt and his father are discussing Miss Crawley's approaching visit and Pitt asks, "What is money compared to our souls, Sir?," his father interprets the remark as an expression of Pitt's disappointment at being left out of her will and of his self-consoling need to feel superior to her. The narrator, however, does not offer an interpretation of Pitt's rhetorical question. Instead, he responds with a question of his own: "and who knows but it *was* Mr. Crawley's meaning?" (10). He provides a certain amount of information, but leaves to *us* the responsibility of making the inference. We are therefore placed in the narrator's position, but his position is that of ours in everyday life, and we are asked to respond to Pitt's statement as we would to that of someone with whom we are familiar and about whose inner life we can make imaginative inferences.

At times the narrator claims only a limited certainty, as when he says: "my belief is [Amelia] made a Confidante of [Laura Martin]" (12). A moment later he remarks: "I know where she kept that packet [of George's letters] she had—and can steal in and out of her chamber like Iachimo," the imaginative villain in Shakespeare's *Cymbelline*. Even momentary omniscience, however—which is all that it can be, following as it does on the heels of limited certainty—can be a betrayal of a character's inmost life, and can therefore be inappropriate to the world of Vanity Fair. Consequently, the narrator imposes an additional restraint upon himself, and consents only to play the role of Moonshine as it is played in Shakespeare's *A Midsummer Night's Dream.*

Three chapters later he alludes to this passage and again self-consciously claims the privilege of "understanding with the omniscience of the novelist" (15). In the earlier passage he had pointed out one kind of limitation upon his use of the convention of authorial omniscience; here he quietly indicates another one: he is only a limited human being, even as a novelist. He needed to have explained to him the basis for Miss Toady's obsequious behavior toward Mrs. Briefless (again, symbolic representatives). Having then understood the veneration that the chance of becoming a baronet's daughter can cause, however, he uses his experience of human nature in Vanity Fair as the basis of his momentarily omniscient understanding of Becky's feelings on having missed the opportunity to become a baronet's wife. In short, the whole concept of omniscience is constantly being evoked in such a way as to limit it.

His dependence upon other people for sources of information, like Dobbin (22) or Dr. Pestler (38), establishes similar limitations, as does his dependence upon Tom Eaves (47), the generic gossip, whom he ironically describes with the impossible epithet: "who knows everything." The "Tomeavesian way" of knowing the world arises from Tom's toadying to prominent people and pretending to know everything about their affairs, down to the last shilling. His "information," therefore, "may or may not be true." Tom Eaves constantly raises possibilities and suggests the existence of mysteries, but most basically he reminds us of the uncertainty of our knowledge.

The narrator, on the other hand, calls our attention to the fact that he is making inferences: "And I dare say she thought" (6); "I'm not sure but that he really thought" (12); "I don't think poor Amelia cared"; "I am not sure that she did not dream" (32); "I don't think they were unhappy" (38); "I am inclined to think" (64). Even when he claims that he "had the good luck to read over Rebecca's shoulder" (25) the note that Rawdon quickly burned, the narrator conveys to us the limitations around a momentary omniscience. He can "no more penetrate or understand [the] mysteries [of female fashion and its customs] than he can know what the ladies talk about when they go up stairs after dinner" (37), but he can discover hints: "It is only by inquiry and perseverance, that one sometimes gets hints of those secrets" and of others in Vanity Fair. That is his task as a novelist and ours as collaborative readers.

Hence, in part, the reason for addressing his readers directly, for his confiding tone, and for his affectionateness. If one is at times implicated in the follies and meannesses of Vanity Fair, and is addressed as "poor parasite and humble hanger-on, . . . you poor rogue" (14), one is also implicated as an involved participant in the narrative process and is therefore addressed as "beloved": "Has the beloved reader . . . never heard similar remarks . . . ?" (12); "Perhaps some beloved female subscriber has arrayed an ass in the splendour and glory of her imagination" (13); "My beloved reader has no doubt in the course of his experience been waylaid by many such a luckless companion" (20); "my respected reader" (23); "You and I, my dear reader, may drop into this condition one day" (38); "my friend in motley" (61); "O brother wearers of motley" (19); "brother" (26); "my brother" (57). In more than one sense, therefore, *Vanity Fair* is "Our history" (25).

Unlike Tom Eaves but like the narrator, we have to evaluate our knowledge and, at appropriate times, to make judgments. He offers guidance, however, when he says: "As I cannot describe the mysteries of freemasonry, although I have a shrewd idea that it is a humbug: so an uninitiated man cannot take upon himself to pourtray the great world accurately, and had best keep his opinions to himself whatever they are" (51). With initiated knowledge and informed judgment—as far as we can attain to them—we can respond to questions like "What *had* happened? Was she guilty or not?" (53). The repetition of such questions in the novel, however, forces us to ask what the questions mean. By being placed in this position, therefore, we find ourselves confronting one of the narrator's most basic assumptions: that humans cannot have moral certainty. Human beings must try to know and try to act responsibly, but need to be constantly aware of the motley that they wear—the motley that defines their essential foolishness, their isolation from each other, and their alienation from the truth, whatever that is.

NARRATIVE COMMENTARY

In "Before the Curtain" the narrator defines himself as "Manager of the Performance," who will, he says later, occasionally "step down from the platform" (8) and comment on the personages in the narrative. His actual mode of commentary, however, is usually much less obtrusive than his metaphor of stepping down from the platform might suggest. In fact, his narrative is suffused with commentary, much of it witty and unobtrusive—often, in fact, an extension of the process of characterization. Commentary and characterization thereby fuse, as we see at the outset of the narrative when he says of Jemima Pinkerton: "In Miss Jemima's eyes an autograph letter of her sister, Miss Pinkerton, was an object of as deep veneration, as would have been a letter from a sovereign" (1). Similarly, he says of her sister: "Miss Pinkerton did not understand French; she only directed those who did."

Such lightheartedly satirical commentary is typically an integral part of the narrative fabric:

> Although schoolmistresses' letters are to be trusted no more nor less than churchyard epitaphs; yet as it sometimes happens that a person departs this life, who is really deserving of all the praises the stone-cutter carves over his bones, who *is* a good Christian, a good parent, child, wife or husband, who actually *does* leave a disconsolate family to mourn his loss— so in academies of the male and female sex it occurs every now and then, that the pupil is fully worthy of the praises bestowed by the disinterested instructor. Now Miss Amelia Sedley was a young lady of this singular species: and deserved not only all that Miss Pinkerton said in her praise, but had many charming qualities which that pompous old Minerva of a woman could not see, from the differences of rank and age between her pupil and herself. (1)

Here as elsewhere the narrator speaks from his characteristic perspective of mature human experience, and with a characteristically evaluative wit that causes us to see the amusing similarity between churchyard and schoolmistresses' exaggerations, and the amusing differences between Amelia and Miss Pinkerton.

His first passage of commentary on Becky develops a metaphor that was to be transformed in the illustrated title page of 1848. Characterizing Becky as a misanthropist, the narrator goes on to examine the implications of her immature attitude: "all the world used her ill said this young misanthropist . . . , and we may be pretty certain that the persons whom all the world treats ill, deserve entirely the treatment they get [*all* is emphatic]. The world is a looking glass and gives back to every man the reflection of his own face—Frown at it and it will look sourly upon you—laugh at it and with it and it is a jolly kind companion" (2). Here he is talking about how to live in the world, but with our knowledge of the melancholy jester looking into a mirror in the 1848 illustration, and of the Manager of the Performance's comment that the general impression one gets from observing Vanity Fair "is one more melancholy than mirthful" ("Before the Curtain"), we realize that to put on a good face in order to live in the world is one thing, but that behind the artifice, the dominant emotion is inevitably somber. If one of the functions of the jester, therefore, is to remind us of our folly, another is to entertain us, to evoke our laughter and briefly overcome the melancholy felt by a contemplative observer of the fair.

The satirical purpose of laughter is the subject of another passage of commentary—the very one, in fact, where the narrator says that he will from time to time emerge from the narrative in order to comment on it. In opposition to the laughter of Becky, whose "laughter comes from one who has no reverence except for prosperity and no eye for anything beyond success," the narrator's laughter exists "to combat and expose such as those" (8). He will not lash human vices in the manner of Swift. Instead he will use laughter to illuminate and satirize human follies—with the implicit hope of all writers of satirical comedy: to foster an attachment to appropriate human values.

Sometimes the satire takes the form of a mock apology, as in the case of Becky's wish to marry Jos simply because of his money. Here the narrator teasingly addresses his commentary to his mature female readers—especially those with unmarried daughters—ironically pretending to justify the crude business of "husband-hunting" (3), which with mock sympathy he refers to as a "task" and as "trouble": "If

Miss Rebecca Sharp had determined in her heart upon making the conquest of this big beau, I don't think, ladies, we have any right to blame her; for though the task of husband-hunting is generally, and with becoming modesty, entrusted by young persons to their Mammas, recollect that Miss Sharp had no kind parent to arrange these delicate matters for her, and that if she did not get a husband for herself, there was no one else in the wide world who would take the trouble off her hands."

Passages like this one can also help us to understand others, like the one where he ironically pretends not to be able to evaluate Becky's claim that she could be a "good" woman if she had £5,000 a year: "And who knows but Rebecca was right in her speculations—and that it was only a question of money and fortune which made the difference between her and an honest woman?" (41). The narrator goes even more deeply into irony shortly thereafter: "'It is all the influence of a long course of Three per Cents,' Becky said to herself, and was right very likely." In case we misread these two passages, however, he soon provides a statement that implicitly identifies the difference between a corrupt materialist like Becky and an honest, if poor woman—a commitment to ethical values—when he refers to "Rebecca, whom we have seen piously praying for Consols" (42). The ethical values implied in this language are grounded in religion, but, as we know and have just seen again, Becky has neither religion nor ethics. Therefore her "speculations" (41) are false. She misreads the basis of the "purer" air and the kindness that she has found in the house of the new Sir Pitt and Lady Jane—as this blended exposition and commentary crucially reveals.

The narrator's commentary also serves importantly to remind us of the passage of time and of the instability of human customs and institutions, of human relationships, and of human life itself. Here again is a source of melancholy, as we see in the passage at the end of number 2 that laments with remarkable concreteness of detail the disappearance of the stagecoach, beginning: "Where is the road now, and its merry incidents of life?" (7). The replacement of the stagecoach by the railroad has meant the disappearance of incidents of *life* because there is no longer any interaction with people living along the road.

Recalling both the details of that life and their embodiment in Dickens's *Pickwick Papers* (another blending of novels and life), the narrator evokes the passing of a whole generation: "Is old Weller alive or dead? and the waiters, yea and the inns at which they waited, and the cold-rounds-of-beef inside, and the stunted ostler, with his blue nose and clinking pail, where is he, and where is his generation?" Coming as it does at the end of the second serial installment, the passage has a special force in reminding us of the evanescence that crucially defines Vanity Fair, and that provides a telling context for Becky, as she moves toward her insubstantial future.

At least 12 deaths occur in the novel, most of them significantly influencing the lives of other people: the deaths of Lady Crawley, Old Sir Pitt, George, Miss Crawley, Mrs. Sedley, Old Sedley, Old Osborne, Pitt Binkie Crawley, Lord Steyne, Jos Sedley, the younger Sir Pitt, and Rawdon. For the narrator, death also permeates the bankruptcy sale of Sedley's possessions, which offers a striking emblem of human evanescence, set amid thoughtless, greedy battles over the material spoils. This spectacle of human folly constitutes an extraordinary "exhibition," as he calls it: "If there is any exhibition in all Vanity Fair which Satire and Sentiment can visit arm in arm together; where you light on the strangest contrasts laughable and tearful: where you may be gentle and pathetic, or savage and cynical with perfect propriety: it is at one of those public assemblies, a crowd of which are advertised every day. . . . There are very few London people, as I fancy, who have not attended at these meetings, and all with a taste for moralising must have thought . . . of the day when their turn shall come too" (17). The "taste for moralising," therefore, derives from the ability to see not only how death defines Vanity Fair, but also how it calls into question the meaning of our human acts and lives. The appropriate response, therefore, is the very mingling of sentiment and satire that permeates the entire narrative.

Both responses are clearly evident in the two images that the narrator presents to us on the occasion of Lady Crawley's death. The first ironically captures the hypocrisy with which death is treated—as emblemized by the hatchment affixed to the front of Sir Pitt's town house. Its social purpose is to *display* the armorial bearings of the deceased person. Rose Dawson had no heraldic arms, however, so the hatchment used on the death of Sir Pitt's mother is dusted off and pressed into service. Even more ironic are the details of what appears underneath the hatchment's coat of arms: the word *Resurgam,* nominally expressing a belief in resurrection ("I shall rise"), "flanked by the Crawley Dove and Serpent" (14), representing the familial hypocrisy and cunning. In Rose's case, the rising was all social, and the narrator responds by remarking how the hatchment offers an opportunity for moralizing. In this case he doesn't do so, presumably because the image itself is so powerfully expressive. He later offers another image that expresses the *pathos* of her life and death, as Sir Pitt kicks open Becky's boxes in a fury at having learned of her marriage to Rawdon and as Rose's children take the clothes and act plays in them: "It was but a few days after the poor mother had gone to her lonely burying-place; and was laid, unwept and disregarded, in a vault full of strangers" (16). To have led a spiritually empty life and to die unloved and unlamented is indeed to be "poor."

Her husband, having degenerated into "a whimpering old idiot put in and out of bed and cleaned and fed like a baby" (40), dies similarly impoverished, having "not a single friend to mourn him" (41). The tone here is darker and even more satirical, as the narrator tells us how "Sir Pitt was forgotten—like the kindest and best of us—only a few weeks sooner," and as he comments on our burial practices: "As long as we have a man's body, we play our Vanities upon it, surrounding it with humbug and ceremonies, laying it in state, and packing it up in gilt nails and velvet; and we finish our duty by placing over it a stone, written all over with lies" (41). Commenting on the analogous monument erected by Old Osborne, with its pretentious imagery, stale Latin quotation, and "pompous Osborne arms" (35), the narrator again points out the impersonality and abstraction of the monument, which lacks any spiritual qualities whatever, even though it has been placed in a church: "The sculptors of those days had stocks of such funereal emblems in hand; as you may see still on the walls of St. Paul's, which are covered with hundreds of these braggart heathen allegories" (35).

These farcical practices and mass-produced works do not express emotion; they are hypocritical pretenses of emotion and inspire some of the narrator's sharpest satire. By contrast, his most intense sympathy seems prompted by people who are weak, or unprotected, or are exploited by others, or who are broken by life. Amelia comes to mind immediately, of course, as the figure who most often calls forth the narrator's sympathy, but she, climactically termed a "tender little parasite" (67), at least is not broken—unlike a number of people whom we see. The condition of young Rawdon, a "poor lonely little benighted boy" (37) living with an unloving mother provokes one of the narrator's most vivid outbursts, while the death of Old Sedley prompts one of his quietest passages of explorative musing as he considers what might be an appropriate ending for a human life.

Here he imagines two contrasting statements representing the archetypal lives of Dives and Lazarus, the rich man and the beggar. The one statement, boastfully articulating worldly success, remains void of spiritual awareness, ending as it does with the empty claim: "I defy any man after I am gone to find anything against my character" (61). The second reveals a man broken by failure, who nevertheless discovers in his very helplessness the basis for a resigned hope: "On my last bed I lie utterly helpless and humble; and I pray forgiveness for my weakness, and throw myself with a contrite heart, at the feet of the Divine Mercy."

As these passages may suggest, we can find in the narrator's commentary a remarkable range of expression: from comical acceptance of human folly to savage criticism of that same folly, and from witty amusement at the entertainments of the Fair to hints of what might lie beyond its limits. As always, however, every statement of the narrator's in *Vanity Fair* is the utterance of a moment—an utterance trapped in the flux of time, and therefore limited. When he refers to himself as the "writer of a history of which every word is true" (62), he is again insisting on the interconnectedness of fiction and truth. At the same time, however, we understand the omnipresent qualification: truth, as far as one can know it.

NARRATIVE TECHNIQUE

In discussing narrative technique, one tends to distinguish between *narrative proper* on the one hand, where the narrator is, as usual, speaking in his own persona, and so-called *scene* on the other, where the narrator presents the imagined language of individual characters speaking directly, as in a drama. Thackerayan narrative, however, exhibits many gradations between the two poles of these complementary aspects of narrative technique. His narrative, therefore, not only varies extensively from tone to tone, but also often moves freely back and forth in time, while his "scenes" can contract into the brevity of a single reported speech. Of course, as we have seen, the narrator himself is a frequently changing entity whose metamorphoses lend themselves to this flexibility of technique.

Because the lives of the narrative's five main characters—Amelia, George, Dobbin, Becky, and Rawdon—often diverge from each other in various ways, and because the narrator wishes to use the resources of the serial novel in order to reveal parallels and contrasts among their lives and the lives of other characters, he frequently employs flashbacks. Perhaps the most obvious of these flashbacks and one of the lengthiest is the one that occurs at the beginning of number 7, where chapter 23, "Captain Dobbin Proceeds on his Canvass," and chapter 24, In "Which Mr. Osborne Takes Down the Family Bible," constitute a single retrospective passage. Number 6 had ended with the arrival of Dobbin in Brighton, bringing two pieces of news from London, one of which he does not tell—the result of his interview with Old Osborne—and the other of which he communicates: that the army has been ordered to Belgium. The lengthy flashback beginning number 7, therefore, supplies the missing information about Dobbin's activities in London: his attempts to conciliate George's sister, his failure to do so with George's father, and the latter's disinheriting of George and furious attempt to disown him.

Even within this flashback, however, we find two further retrospective passages—brief, but significant. In the first of these, as Old

Osborne withdraws into his study, we learn about the history of that room, into which "No member of the household, child or domestic, had ever entered . . . without a certain terror. . . . George as a boy had been horsewhipped in this room many times; his mother sitting sick on the stair listening to the cuts of the whip . . . ; the poor woman used to fondle and kiss him secretly, and give him money to soothe him when he came out" (24). Even more shatteringly, the narrator focuses upon a picture painted years before of young George, his two sisters, and his mother, "simpering on each other in the approved family-portrait manner. The mother lay under ground now, long since forgotten—the sisters and brother had a hundred different interests of their own, and, familiar still, were utterly estranged from each other."

This passage gives us in effect a mini-history of the human family, with its brutality, self-deception, and alienation—a picture of masked ugliness that calls forth one of the narrator's most vehement comments: "what bitter satire there is in those flaunting childish family-portraits, with their farce of sentiment and smiling lies, and innocence so self-conscious and self-satisfied." What reader can fail to see how effectively this passage of retrospection deepens our understanding of what Old Osborne is doing? What he is doing and trying to do, of course, is an act of archetypal ugliness: not only to disinherit but to obliterate his son, as we see when he takes down his pompous scarlet and gilt Bible (from its position next to the *Peerage*) and cancels George's name—thereby reenacting Abraham's willingness to kill Isaac, as depicted on the Bible's frontispiece.

Between the time of his entering the study and his obliteration of George's name, however, comes a second retrospective passage that provides us with a further understanding of what he is about to do and of what he feels. After he locks the door of the room, we see him "turning over . . . and musing over" the "memorials" of George— from copybooks, early letters, requests for money, and receipted bills, to a lock of his hair—and then recalling a hundred images of George kept within his memory, even as he feels "pangs of sickening rage, balked ambition and love; . . . wounds of outraged vanity, tenderness even." Here again is an archetypal situation: like Dante's Francesca in the *Inferno*, Old Osborne feels "that bitterest of all helpless woe, with which miserable men think of happy past times." This second retrospective passage, therefore, complicates our understanding by giving us a further perspective on Old Osborne's action, and by evoking its pathos as well as its folly.

This same installment (number 7), moreover, has further narrative complications. After the major flashback of chapters 23 and 24 has ended and the narrative of Dobbin in Brighton with George, Amelia, Becky, Rawdon, and Jos continues, the narration moves back in time twice more, calling forth a notable comment to the reader, saying that "Our history is destined in this Chapter to go backwards and forwards in a very irresolute manner seemingly," but offering justification: "so that the whole of the tale may get a hearing" (25). The first retrospective passage explains how Becky has been captivating George in Brighton and making Amelia uneasy after only seven days of marriage. What the narrator calls "a little trifling disarrangement and disorder" in the narrative, therefore, ironically reflects the disarrangement and disorder in Amelia's marriage, not to mention Becky's. The second passage of retrospection then clarifies several references to Miss Crawley's presence in Brighton, by picking up this strand of the narrative and bringing us up to date by explaining how the domineering reign of Mrs. Bute came to an end. It thereby prepares for the installment's conclusion, where Rawdon and Becky, drawn to London by the promise of money, receive only £20 from Miss Crawley's banker.

Retrospective passages occur much earlier in the novel, of course, beginning in chapter 2. Because Thackeray likes to have striking dramatic scenes in the opening chapters of his novels, the immediately ensuing chapters typically offer us retrospection that helps to account for what we have witnessed. After seeing Becky's departing battle with Miss Pinkerton and her rejection of the *Dictionary*, therefore, we learn in the second chapter, through narrative and commentary, about the past history of the girl and about the reasons for her behavior in the previous chapter. Similarly, in chapter 3 we first see Jos in a scene, and then learn about him and his past—understandably, in a passage of retrospection. The narrator suspends this practice in the rest of the first installment, however—notably in the case of

George Osborne, about whom we receive only little scraps of information, but on the other hand he devotes most of the opening chapter of the second installment to a retrospective passage that provides a basis for understanding George by evoking his childhood self. More notably, perhaps, the narrator also uses the flashback to introduce the final major character, Dobbin, about whom we have not previously even heard, showing us the affectionate, hero-worshipping basis of his attachment to George.

The fourth major retrospection occurs at the opening of chapter 7, where—having previously met Sir Pitt in a scene with Becky, and learned about him through his confidences to her as well as from his own behavior—we are given the history of his politically syco-phantic family. Most unusually, however, the chapter—and the number with it—ends with retrospection. On this occasion the narration does not concern itself with an individual character or family, but with the passage of time itself, as emblemized by the disappearance of the stagecoach—thereby providing a larger context for those individual lives.

During the next flashback, which begins number 3, the narrator effaces himself by having Becky report to Amelia on her reception at Queen's Crawley, an account that animatedly moves back and forth between Becky's observations and the reported language of others, whom we therefore meet scenically: Lady Crawley and Pitt, especially, but also Horrocks and, at the very end, Miss Horrocks, who is anonymously introduced as a woman "very much overdressed, and who flung me a look of great scorn" (8). The narrator, having reestablished his presence and his values with a passage of commentary at the chapter's end about Becky's account, then goes on to use immediately subsequent flashbacks as a means of providing needed information about these family members. Chapter 9, Family Portraits, therefore, examines the history of Lady Crawley and of Pitt before providing a further characterization of Sir Pitt, and ends with three pointed sentences that tell us about the existence of his wealthy, unmarried sister, Miss Crawley, whose money is to be the focus of so much attention, "for she had a balance at her banker's which would have made her beloved anywhere" (9).

Here again the flashback begets a passage of commentary, as the narrator ends the chapter by projecting two complementary images. The first emphasizes the archetypal nature of the situation in which Miss Crawley finds herself, and of the greedy, toadying responses of others to the wealth of a relative. Implicating the reader as well as himself, not just the other Crawleys, he remarks: "How tenderly we look at her faults if she is a relative (and may every reader have a score of such)! What a kind good-natured old creature we find her!" The comically exaggerated parenthetical remark, however, leads inevitably to his demonstration of how we satirize ourselves when we create such fastasies and to his bifurcated conclusion: "Sweet sweet vision! Foolish foolish dream." The second image faces us directly with an analogous bifurcation: the famous drawing of the seated jester with the melancholy Thackerayan face holding the grinning comic mask. These two emblematic images, therefore—as evoked successively by language and by literal picture—serve not only to reveal a paradigm of human behavior, and to remind us of the narrator's continuing presence with us in Vanity Fair, but also to characterize the folly of the scheming that is to ensue, as people seek Miss Crawley's money.

Naturally, we have to learn about Miss Crawley, but she does not appear in a scene for a considerable time because the narrator wishes to place emphasis on the relationships of other people to her. His handling of the major flashback regarding her is rather unusual, therefore, for his presentation of her past is subtly intermingled with his reporting of brief utterances that typify the attitudes of her relatives toward her and toward her partiality for Rawdon. Thus, for example, as soon as we learn that she has £70,000, has almost adopted Rawdon, and despises the sanctimonious Pitt, we hear language that typifies Pitt's self-justifying response: "'She is a godless woman of the world,' would Mr. Crawley say. 'She lives with atheists and Frenchmen. My mind shudders when I think of her awful awful situation, and that near as she is to the grave, she should be so given up to vanity, licentiousness, profaneness, and folly'" (10).

Similarly, later in this retrospective narrative, when we learn about her silly approval of Rawdon's duels, "in which he gave ample proofs of his contempt for death," the narrator interjects a typical verbal response of Pitt's that is almost a dramatic reply to the narrator's own language: "'And for what follows after death,' would Mr. Crawley observe, throwing his gooseberry eyes up to the ceiling. He was always thinking of his brother's soul or of the souls of those who differed with him in opinion—it is a sort of comfort which many of the serious give themselves." We then hear Miss Crawley's first reported language, as the narrator gives us her typical reply: "'[Rawdon] will sow his wild-oats,' she would say, 'and is worth far more than that puling hypocrite of a brother of his.'" We perceive, therefore, that the flashback does more than simply provide significant information about one person, since it also shows us various relationships, gives us characteristic language of the people involved, almost as if in a conversation, and provokes generalizing commentary.

This particular flashback unobtrusively continues into the beginning of chapter 11, where we learn about Bute Crawley and his wife, who have been only briefly mentioned up to now. Here too we have narration interspersed with the brief utterances of individual characters—both typifying language, like Bute's "'hang it' (as he would say), 'Matilda *must* leave me half her money'" (11), or the language of a specific occasion, like that of Mrs. Bute's prying letter to Miss Pinkerton, followed by Becky's second letter to Amelia. It is in Becky's letter, moreover, that we hear for the second time Miss Crawley's own actual language: "'When I come into the country,' she says (for she has a great deal of humour), 'I leave my toady, Miss Briggs, at home—My brothers are my toadies here, my dear'" (11)—a statement reinforced by the illustration, *Miss Crawley's affectionate relatives*.

By the time we come to the end of Becky's letter and hear a new passage of narration about Mrs. Bute and her husband, soon followed by a dramatic scene, we do not know with certainty where we are in narrative time, so subtle is the narrator's handling of it. We seem to be a kind of continuum where the immediate past and the present blend, as we hear the appalling but amusing conversation between the cleric and his wife speculating upon Miss Crawley's death with comments like: "I think she's going," and "I lay five to two Matilda drops in a year." Only thereafter do we hear conversations in which Miss Crawley is actually engaged—revealingly, not with relatives, but with Becky—but these conversations also take place in a generalized continuum, which continues up to the end of the chapter (and number).

By the time of number 4, narrative flashback does not function to introduce us to the past lives of characters whom we have just met, or whom we are about to meet. Rather, it serves to characterize the lives of Amelia and George during the year or year and a half that Becky has spent at Queen's Crawley, to tell us of the decline in Old Sedley's fortunes, to dramatize the increasing hostility of Old Osborne, and to remind us of military events in Europe. Chapters 12, "Quite a Sentimental Chapter," and 13, "Sentimental and Otherwise," therefore, take us up to the time when the narratives focusing upon Amelia and Becky once more join in the present, as Miss Crawley returns to London under the care of Becky. Shifts away from an active line of development such as Becky's involvement with the Crawleys, however, tend to leave a narrative gap, so that a subsequent flashback is needed—in this case a passage in the middle of chapter 14 to show us the responses to Miss Crawley's illness at Queen's Crawley, the development of Rawdon's infatuation with Becky, and her continuing ability to rout his clumsy approaches.

Similarly, a narrative focus on the marital result of his infatuation and her failure to understand Miss Crawley, on their social interaction with George and Amelia, and on the outraged responses of Sir Pitt and Miss Crawley to the news of the marriage, leaves a gap in our awareness of the consequences of Old Sedley's monetary difficulties. Accordingly, the narrative of the sordid auction of his household goods in chapter 17 requires the retrospective account of how it came to be—an account that soon turns into the recapitulation of the newly married life of Becky and Rawdon, who, of course, have no more money than the bankrupt Sedleys, and who face the threat of a similar future.

Because Old Sedley's ruin was in part caused by the reemergence of Napoleon as a military threat, a recapitulation of those important developments also requires a passage of retrospective narration, which initiates chapter 18. Emphasizing the destructive effects of politics and warfare upon the lives of the Sedley family, it leads to an account of how the father's bankruptcy caused the end of Amelia's engagement and of how George's regiment has been ordered abroad. These are indeed threats to her well-being, but so is the marriage itself, as a remarkable retrospective passage in chapter 26 demonstrates. Here it is Amelia herself who, after only nine days of marriage, looks back sadly as well as fondly to "that image of George to which she had knelt before marriage" (26). She cannot consciously admit to herself "how different the real man was from that superb young hero whom she had worshipped," but she knows it emotionally—which is why she feels "wounded" and sad. Here her life epitomizes life in Vanity Fair, dominated and misled by false expectations of happiness.

The narrator continues to use flashbacks when introducing characters like the O'Dowds (27), General Tufto (28), Lady Jane (33), and of course Lord Steyne, who receives a whole chapter (47). Passages of retrospection also serve to recapitulate developments like the degeneration of Sir Pitt after the news of Becky's marriage (33), or Becky's success in settling with Rawdon's creditors so that he and she can return to London (36), or her demoralization during her vagabond life on the Continent (64). Two flashbacks devoted to young Rawdon, however, deserve special mention, for they pointedly and memorably epitomize not only his situation in the household, but also a crucial development in his relationship with his mother.

The first retrospection evokes the wonderful relationship between father and son, who play together and are "great friends" (37), and the sharply contrasting, one-sided relationship between the largely absent mother and the lonely son, who in response creates a touchingly unreal image of her. Her splendid clothing, jewels, and perfumes (none of which have been paid for) help make her into "an unearthly being in his eyes . . . : to be worshipped and admired at a distance. To drive with that lady in the carriage was an awful rite: he sate up in the back seat, and did not dare to speak: he gazed with all his eyes at the beautifully dressed princess opposite to him." When he walks into her room while she is away, it seems like "the abode of a fairy to him"—the robes, the silver-clasped jewel case, and even what to us seems rather chilling: "the mystic bronze hand on the dressing-table, glistening all over with a hundred rings."

His next appearance also comes in a retrospective passage—one that directly recalls the former. Here we see him after almost two years have passed: "He was a fine open faced boy, with blue eyes and waving flaxen hair, sturdy in limb, but generous and soft in heart: fondly attaching himself to all who were good to him. . . . The beautiful mother-vision had faded away after a while. During near two years she had scarcely spoken to the child. She disliked him. He had the measles and the hooping-cough. He bored her" (44). Most revealingly of all, however, as she suddenly discovers him outside the door of the drawing room where she is singing to Lord Steyne, she loses control of herself and boxes him on the ear for being a "spy" upon her and Steyne—raising the question: "What is their secret?" We notice, moreover, that her vehemence continues, as her "dislike increased to hatred," and that "Steyne also heartily misliked the boy," prompting the boy to square his fists at Steyne's hat out in the hall. By means of this memorable incident involving young Rawdon, therefore, the narrator raises the question of Becky's guilt, and tells us that the servants have "pronounced against her."

One might anticipate the appearance of flashbacks in order to explain developments in the lives of Jos after Waterloo, and of Dobbin and Amelia (38), or of Old Osborne (42), or to explain the presence of Briggs in Curzon Street (40). More notable use of retrospective narration, however, can be seen in two final examples. The first occurs as Becky and Rawdon revisit Queen's Crawley for the first time. The narrator could have given us a totally sequential account of their arrival and of the events that ensued. Instead, however, he makes a point of introducing a brief retrospective passage in order to call attention to a particular event. Part of the way through the narrative, therefore, he stops and tells us: "But before this, Lady Jane conducted Rebecca to the apartments prepared for her . . . and asked her sister-in-law in what more she could be useful" (41). Becky, revealingly, asks to see "your dear little children"—not because she likes children, as we know, but because she wants to evaluate the health of the future baronet (if he lives that long): Pitt Binkie Crawley, who proves, to her satisfaction, to be a "pale, heavy-eyed" boy overdosed with medicine. Passages like this help form our picture of Becky as relentlessly purposeful—always flattering, always cajoling, always calculating. Instead of *telling* us what is in her mind, however, the narrator has pointedly *shown* us.

The second example is furnished by chapter 52, "In Which Lord Steyne Shows Himself in a Most Amiable Light"—an unmistakably ironic title for a chapter that comes to show *him* cajoling and calculating. The full meaning of the irony becomes only slowly apparent, however, because the language continues for a time in that mode: "When Lord Steyne was benevolently disposed, he did nothing by halves, and his kindness towards the Crawley family did the greatest honour to his benevolent discrimination. His lordship extended his good-will to little Rawdon"—the same little Rawdon whom we know him to mislike heartily. After having the boy sent away to school, therefore, "Lord Steyne, who took such a parental interest in the affairs of this amiable poor family, thought that their expenses might be very advantageously curtailed by the departure of Miss Briggs." Unlike some other passages of retrospection, this chapter reveals its purpose only gradually, especially with the phrase, "Little Rawdon being disposed of," and then with the phrase, "so two of Rawdon's out-sentinels were in the hands of the enemy." In addition, however, the chapter eventually comes to reveal the meaning of the previous chapter's ending, for we finally understand clearly that Wenham proposed a walk home with Rawdon so that the bailiffs would seize him, thereby removing the third obstacle in Steyne's path.

A number of other retrospective passages exist in the novel, helping to form its complex series of interrelationships, to enhance its variety, to deepen our understanding of the narrative, and to provide striking insight into its characters, whether the retrospection be expressed in the language of the narrator himself, or in the language of one of his personages—as in a letter, or in a document like young George's essay "On Selfishness," the wonderfully ironic implications of which neither he nor his mother understand. Other aspects of narrative technique, however, also call for comment, especially the relationship between scene and narrative proper.

Except for Chapter 8, which opens with a narrative letter from Becky to Amelia, all of *Vanity Fair*'s chapters begin with observations by the narrator rather than with a dramatic scene. Forty percent of the chapters *end* with a scene, or with a scene capped by a brief remark of commentary, however, as do slightly more than one-half of the serial installments. The first serial installment is notable in this regard, for it is unique in having all four chapters end scenically. The first, of course, ends with Becky's rejection of the *Dictionary*, as illustrated by *Rebecca's Farewell,* and capped by the narrator's remark: "The world is before the two young ladies; and so farewell to Chiswick Mall." The remaining chapters of the first installment all end with reported language, as Amelia tells Becky not to be frightened on entering the drawing room (2), as Mrs. Sedley comments on the departing Jos, "Poor Joe, why *will* he be so shy?" (3), and as we hear two complementary utterances: Amelia's comment to Becky that she is sure Jos will propose, and Jos's comment to himself, "Gad, I'll pop the question at Vauxhall" (4).

Other notable scenic endings occur at the conclusion of number 3, with its mingled speech and commentary about Becky being a match for father and son (11), of Number 4, "Oh, Sir—I—I'm *married already*" (14), of number 5, where George proposes to Amelia, of number 7, where Rawdon reports receiving only £20 from Miss Crawley's lawyer (25), and of number 12, where Osborne's daughter tells him that she has seen young George and the old man begins "to tremble in every limb" (42). Only two other scenic chapter endings stand out, both of them within installments: George's angry resolve to defy his father, as expressed in his comment to Dobbin, "'I'll marry her tomorrow,' he said with an oath. 'I love her more every day, Dobbin'" (21), and the arrest of Rawdon by the bailiffs (51), reinforced by the illustration, *Colonel Crawley is wanted.* Considering the length of this narrative, one finds these scenic endings to be relatively few in number, and not always purely scenic. For more characteristic endings, therefore, one must turn to passages of narrative or of narrative commentary.

Here one recalls especially the ending of number 2, with its commentary on the transitoriness of human customs and human life (7)—a passage that establishes a fundamentally prevailing tone in the narrative. Only two of the serial endings concern themselves with notable dramatic events: in number 8, where Brussels awakes to the sound of the army marching to battle (29), and in number 9, where darkness comes down on the city and on the field where George lies dead (32). Otherwise, chapter and number endings concern themselves with the lesser events appropriate to "this domestic comedy of Vanity Fair" (18), and with quiet or occasionally satirical reflections upon them.

Thus we hear the narrator's reflections upon his role and the role of laughter (8), the unwitting self-satire of our hopes for money from wealthy relatives (9), learn of the identity of Becky's husband (15), the approaching death of Miss Crawley—an especially gentle ending (34), Dobbin's departure for India (35), the meeting of little George and little Rawdon (37), Briggs's lending £600 to Becky and Rawdon (40), Becky's secreting of the £1,000 note from Steyne (48), the narrator's comments on the collapse of Becky's schemes (53), Dobbin's feelings on returning to England (58), and the death of Steyne (64). As this may suggest, quiet passages of narration tend to conclude the chapters and increasingly characterize later serial installments, numbers 8, 11, 14, 18, and 19–20 being made up entirely of chapters with narrative endings. As this suggests, the prevailing impression left upon readers by the narrative is not of a series of *climactic* scenic or narrative events, though such events indeed occur; to a much greater extent we recall a series of quietly interwoven speeches, reports, and comments that constantly vary in proportion to one another in accordance with the narrator's purposes.

7

Style and Substance

If one of the origins of style is the impulse to imitate, another can be the wish to parody—a motive quite strong in Thackeray's narrator. We see it at some length near the beginning of chapter 6, where he exemplifies how he might have written "in the genteel, or in the romantic, or in the facetious manner," but it made its appearance long before that, near the beginning of chapter 1: "'Have you completed all the necessary preparations incident to Miss Sedley's departure, Miss Jemima?' asked Miss Pinkerton herself, that majestic lady: the Semiramis of Hammersmith, the friend of Doctor Johnson, the correspondent of Mrs. Chapone herself." He uses Miss Pinkerton's own language to introduce her and the language reveals her pompous formality, especially in her use of "incident to" and "Miss" Jemima (who has just addressed her as "sister").

Her sister's simple language and her own contrasting language, therefore, give us an immediate sense of this woman, but the narrator's parodic language provides us with the telling comic *evaluation*. By repeating the emphatic word "herself," by listing her apparent honors or accomplishments, but especially by using the phrase "the Semiramis of Hammersmith," the narrator comically renders her sense of superiority and at the same time creates the basis for our mocking laughter because Semiramis was a mythical queen of Assyria famous for her wisdom and prudence—an image of majesty too great to be contained within Miss Pinkerton's language or being, or within the mundane world of this little suburban English village, Hammersmith. His language is therefore mock-heroic, being meant to show the discrepancy between Miss Pinkerton's language and personality on the one hand, and visionary magnificence on the other.

Indeed, mock-heroic language serves as a major vehicle of the narrator's satire, beginning with his introductory promise in "Before the Curtain" that we will witness "some dreadful combats, some grand and lofty horse-riding . . . brilliantly illuminated with the Author's own candles." Here again, his illustration of the serial cover provides immediate illumination, for the jester and his audience exist in a mock-heroic setting as defined by the presence of two comical statues: one of a figure riding a long-eared, asslike creature set atop a triumphal arch, apparently inspired by a contemporary statue of the Duke of Wellington in London, and the other of a figure standing on his head atop a tall column, apparently inspired by another contemporary monument to another hero of Napoleonic warfare, Lord Nelson—the famous monument in Trafalgar Square that had been erected in 1843. The lath sword carried by the boy looking up at the jester reappears on the later title page of what is now called "A Novel without a Hero," where it has become the jester's own weapon. Additionally, the cocked hat worn by the boy reappears in the initial vignette of chapter 5, illustrating a mock battle between two boys, one of whom is mounted on a horse; chapter 5, of course, narrates the "long . . . remembered" fight between Cuff and Dobbin. Finally, the paper hat has its counterpart in the narrative as a literal military cocked hat, like the one illustrated later in the chapter, which is dropped by Dobbin as he bows to Amelia, making her "one of the clumsiest bows that was ever performed by a mortal"—more mock-heroic language.

In short, these mock-heroic pictorial images and the language that supplements them intimately connect the worlds of history and of fiction, making Napoleonic Europe a part of Vanity Fair, and presenting warfare not only as a literal fact, but also as a metaphor for a great deal of human conduct. Napoleon himself exists in the narrative only in the ironic form of an "august mute personage" (18), who is characterized merely in terms of his impact on the characters of the narrative. Becky is the first to mention him, doing so in the context of her successful use of French in her "little battle" (1) with Miss Pinkerton, after which she cries: "thank Heaven for French. *Vive la France! Vive l'Empereur! Vive Bonaparte!*"—thereby, of course, shocking Amelia by praising such an ominous, threatening figure.

The narrator intermittently reminds us of Napoleon's presence and of major military events connected with him (chapters 5, 6, 7, 9, 12, and 13), but typically in a comic manner. To the materialistically successful Sedley, he is just "Boney" (3), a possessor of fine champagne. The battle of Borodino simply becomes the occasion for "a savage cantata against the Corsican Upstart, who had lately met with his Russian reverses" (6), performed by Mrs. Salmon "under the gilt cockle-shell" of the Vauxhall pleasure gardens. The battle of Prague also reemerges in musical form as George's sisters play the piece, but only succeed in provoking him: "'Stop that d—— thing,' George howled out in a fury from the sofa. 'It makes me mad'" (21). Vauxhall's grand panorama of Moscow, in turn, merely serves as a setting for Becky's own campaign against Jos (also doomed to fail).

The narrator simulates the language of newspapers of 1813 to point out the vast scale and immense destructiveness of Napoleonic warfare: "Battle of Leipsic, six hundred thousand men engaged, total defeat of the French, two hundred thousand killed" (12). The narrator's mocking perspective on this senseless slaughter, however, reminds us that the news affects not just "all the hearts" but also "all the Stocks of Europe," and tells us that "the retreat from Leipsic made no difference in the number of meals Mr. Sambo took in the Servants' Hall—the allies poured into France and the dinner bell rang at five o'clock just as usual—I don't think poor Amelia . . . was fairly interested in the war until the abdication of the Emperor."

After his abdication, as the narrator speaks in the protective accents of Amelia's mind and feelings, Napoleon is "the Corsican monster locked up at Elba" (13), no longer threatening George. Even upon Napoleon's return from exile, however, his importance in the narrative derives from his effect upon Old Sedley and Amelia: "in the month of March, Anno Domini 1815, Napoleon landed at Cannes, and Louis XVIII. fled, and all Europe was in alarm, and the funds fell, and old John Sedley was ruined" (18). Only the mention of "old John Sedley" arouses our sympathies, and if he is raised to a wry importance by being mentioned in this series, Napoleon is at the same time belittled by having his significance reduced to his effect upon a London speculator.

To the embittered, ruined Sedley he is "that Corsican scoundrel from Elba" (20), "that infernal traitor Bonaparty" (26). To the terrified Jos at Brussels, he is "Napoleon! What warrior was there, however famous and skilful, that could fight at odds with him?" (32). To the reader, however, these are comical enlargements, especially Jos's statement, which is a fantasy produced by his terror—all the more evident in the light of *our* knowledge that Wellington is just about to defeat Napoleon at Waterloo. Such language, therefore, has an ironic force that is directed not only against the speaker but also against the object of his anger or fear. In short, all these attitudes toward Napoleon help to define and differentiate character, but whether hateful, scornful, patronizing, or simply fearful, they also serve to reduce his size.

The only person besides Becky who praises Napoleon is the mercenary Pitt Crawley, who does so in order to toady to his wealthy Whiggish aunt after Rawdon's fall from favor. When the Dowager Countess of Southdown belabors "the Corsican upstart" (34) with elaborately exaggerated language, Pitt speaks up in favor of the person whom the narrator ironically calls "the man of Destiny"—the term once used to account for Napoleon's apparent invincibility, but no longer adequate following his final, utter defeat. Pitt's language of praise is as ludicrously exaggerated as Lady Southdown's disparagement, as he speaks "in terms of the strongest indignation of the faithless conduct of the allies toward this dethroned monarch, who, after giving himself generously up to their mercy, was consigned to an ignoble and cruel banishment, while a bigoted Popish rabble was tyrannising over France in his stead." In short, the narrative presentation of Napoleon continues to be ironic.

Nor is Wellington immune to such treatment. The public images resulting from his popularity call forth only ironic laughter from the narrator, who mocks the "Achilles" statue of Wellington, and "the hideous equestrian monster" (22) on the Green Park arch that prompted the mock-heroic image on the serial cover. Hero worship is not made admirable by being British. Similarly, mention of Wellington's campaign on the Iberian peninsula occurs in the ironic context of news that Dobbin's Regiment of Foot has "returned from yellow fever in the West Indies, to which the fortune of the service had ordered his regiment, while so many of his gallant comrades were reaping glory in the Peninsula" (5).

"Glory," however, is just an inflated abstraction in this narrative—little more than the subject of dinnertime chat at a speculator's table in Russell Square: "They talked about war and glory and Boney and Lord Wellington and the last Gazette." Mention of the *London Gazette*, an official paper containing legal and goverment notices, including bankruptcies, pensions, and promotions, provides a final irony because it is associated in the narrative less with success than with financial failure and death. It will announce the ruin of Sedley—in whose very house the conversation is taking place—and the death of one of the conversation's participants: George. The sentence, therefore, proceeds along a path of constant diminishment: from the magnitude of war and the false magnitude of "glory," to the two "august" personages who direct the slaughter, to the most transient accounts of their pawns and victims. The Englishmen who write these perishable newspaper accounts, however, do not share the narrator's more comprehensive outlook. Instead, they speak in inflated epic terms of "the genius of the immortal Wellington!" (26). Therefore, when the narrator momentarily adopts this tone and speaks of Waterloo as "the greatest event of history" (28), we instantly recognize the newspaperlike exaggeration and understand how the mocking irony applies to Wellington as well as to Napoleon.

The references to Wellington reach a climax in chapter 29. Just as the narrator had previously measured Napoleon's importance by his effect upon a suffering girl, so here too he presents Wellington with similar belittling indirection. Wellington is mentioned only as part of a group in the center of which is Becky, and his presence is announced in the *patois* of Mrs. O'Dowd: "'Sure, it's the Juke himself,' cried Mrs. O'Dowd to Jos, who began to blush violently" (29). As usual, the manner of the narrative presentation is crucial. Wellington serves only to call forth the comically inflated social vanity of Mrs. O'Dowd, who claims to be related to him, and of Jos, who claims to have known him in India, where they both danced with Miss Cutler. In the narrative he literally exists only as the vanity of vanities, and in this he is joined, though somewhat differently, by Napoleon.

The Napoleonic wars receive similar treatment from the very start, being introduced in the parodic form of the schoolboy battle between Cuff and Dobbin, where the mock-heroic style raises a number of issues that have serious importance in the narrative as a whole. As the battle reaches its climax, the narrator pauses to provide us with a series of ironic perspectives that prompt a larger understanding. By wishing for the skill of "a Napier or a Bell's Life" (5), he pretends to need the lofty abilities of a military historian like Sir William Napier, author of a vast *History of the War in the Peninsula,* or the down-to-earth abilities of a reporter for a sporting newspaper such as *Bell's Life in London.* He then evokes the Napoleonic wars in terms of their climactic event, doing so by parodying narratives of military history, and then replacing this language with that of sports reportage:

> It was the last charge of the Guard (that is it *would* have been, only Waterloo had not yet taken place). It was Ney's column breasting the hill of La Haye Sainte, bristling with ten thousand bayonets and crowned with twenty eagles—It was the shout of the beef-eating British, as leaping down the hill they rushed to hug the enemy in the savage arms of Battle—in other words, Cuff coming up full of pluck but quite reeling and groggy, the Fig-merchant put in his left as usual on his adversary's nose and sent him down for the last time.
>
> "I think *that* will do for him," Figs said, as his opponent dropped as neatly on the green as I have seen Jack Spot's ball plump into the pocket at billiards. (5)

Besides the stylistic parody, which mocks the enthusiasm of military narratives, we note the effects produced by the deliberately anachronistic use of time, and by the ironic perspective that time provides. Because the narrator insists upon the anachronism, he emphasizes our need to understand each event in terms of the other, and he implicitly proclaims the superiority of the narrative perspective over the narrated events. This in turn implies the need for an emotionally and temporally distant perspective. As the comical reference to billiards implies, war and fistfighting are not appropriate subjects of enthusiastic admiration. If we can see each of them—from an emotionally distant perspective—as a game, we can understand that it is not harmless, but a game of crazed opponents. So too, as we look back upon events—in the case of Waterloo, one of more than 30 years for readers of 1847, one of almost 180 for readers of today—the temporally lengthening perspective colors past events with a deep tinge of futility. The famous battle of Waterloo is vanity and so is the "famous combat" between Cuff and Dobbin as seen from the perspective of time.

More immediately, of course, the Cuff-Dobbin battle has a certain significance: Cuff is awakened to his responsibility, Dobbin's miserable isolation is over, and the little society is temporarily freed from a young tyrant. Nevertheless, a schoolboy battle fought before an audience of applauding toadies with rapidly shifting loyalties (like the Belgians) is not only an analogue of Waterloo, but also a remote cause, as is a boxing match, another form of licenced violence. When the narrator pictures the victorious British rushing after the defeated French "to hug the enemy in the savage arms of Battle," by ironically expressing a mass, impersonal urge to kill in terms of an individual gesture of personal love, he suggests that this warlike craze to kill is an act of perversion, a denial of our capacity to love and of the very meaning of love. The mock-heroic style of this narrative account, therefore, provides an evaluative context for judging all human warfare, both literal and metaphoric.

The Cuff-Dobbin combat is vanity because of its temporality. The toadies will continue in their ways, and new bullies and dandies will soon spring up to take the place of a Cuff, as the narrator indicates by once again joining novels and life: "Your children will so do and be done by in all probability." So too when the post-Waterloo epoch takes on a latter-day reality, we see that the chief legacy of its initiatory event is hatred, as the narrator firmly emphasizes, just before he summarizes the battle's ending: "[The French] pant for an opportunity of revenging that humiliation; and if a contest, ending in a victory on their part, should ensue, elating them in their turn, and leaving its cursed legacy of hatred and rage behind to us, there is no end to the so-called glory and shame, and to the alternations of successful and unsuccessful murder, in which two high-spirited nations might engage" (32). Such "glory and shame" are mere illusions. The reality is murder.

As the mock-heroic language indicates, therefore, Waterloo is a magnified version of the childhood combats that seem so universal. At Eton warfare extends to brothers; in spite of Pitt's diplomacy "his younger brother Rawdon used to lick him violently" (9). At Queen's Crawley Becky permits the "constant battles" (10) of her pupils, disarmingly but unrealistically named Rose and Violet—as depicted, for example, in the illustration *Miss Sharp in her Schoolroom*. When little Rawdon goes to school, his father learns again all about "school, and fights, and fagging" (52). Old Osborne loves to hear that young George has been engaging in what the narrator calls "war" (56) by "wopping" other boys: "English youth have been so educated time out of mind, and we have hundreds of thousands of apologists and admirers of injustice, misery, and brutality, as perpetratated among children."

Here, chapters and years after the Cuff-Dobbin battle, we just have more of the same human conduct. With such an educational system and with such encouraging "adult" human attitudes, it is little wonder that warring upon one's fellow humans becomes general in life. As a contrast, we notice that Dobbin voluntarily becomes George's servant at school: "he was his valet, his dog, his man-Friday" (5). The motive is love, "such a love and affection as is only felt by children," but the naïveté of the love, its human self-debasement ("his dog"), and the unworthiness of the childish love's object all suggest that there is an inherent fallacy in the act of glorifying another human being.

If the Cuff-Dobbin battle establishes a major connection between the world of childhood aggression and warfare, so too, as we have previously seen, the scenes in Brussels establish a similar connection between adult social aggression and the adjacent military conflict.

Cuff's sense of a battle as a kind of dance, prompts the "contemptuous smile on his face," as he delivers his blows in a manner "as light and as gay as if he was at a ball." Correspondingly, one of the most brilliant aspects of the great (literal) ball at Brussels on the eve of Waterloo, where Becky treats Amelia so contemptuously, and where George fantasizes so extravagantly about his abilities as a conqueror, lies in its ability to stimulate our awareness not only of its contrast with the next day's warfare, but also of its likeness thereto. These adjacent civilian and military worlds are intimately analogous. Metaphorically speaking, one sees them governed by similar motives, marked by similar triumphs, and shaken by similar defeats, for in them nation is turned against nation, human against human, and familial flesh against familial flesh—the extended family being, of course, the family of mankind.

The centrality of the Napoleonic analogies appears with special emphasis in the case of Becky. As we have seen, her most effective weapon against Miss Pinkerton is her use of her "mother tongue" (2), which she also uses to praise France and *l'Empereur*. In the closed little cage of Chiswick, she seems like an "eagle," the predatory threatening bird of war that "crowned" (5) the battle emblems of Napoleon. Like the diminutive "Corsican upstart" (6, 34), she is "a little upstart" (6), an outsider trying to rise to lofty heights. She is in fact a female Napoleon, a clever, calculating, aggressive, ruthless leader who excites great interest and certain kinds of often frantic devotion in the men around her, from old Sir Pitt and Rawdon to Jos, George, Pitt, and Steyne. Rawdon "believed in his wife as much as the French soldiers in Napoleon" (34). Before leaving for the war she dictates a letter to his aunt, "marching up and down the room with her hands behind her" (25), dictating her words in an martial manner, and then, preparing for a possible skirmish with the landlord, sends their valuables away with George's servant, "as a general sends his baggage to the rear before an action." In Brussels she is equally masterful: "'If the worst comes to the worst,' Becky thought, 'my retreat is secure; and I have a right-hand seat in the barouche'" (31). Pitt vows that Becky is "fit to be the wife of an Emperor" (44), and when she goes to court, she acts like one: "She walked into the royal apartments with a toss of the head which would have befitted an empress, and . . . had she been one, she would have become the character perfectly" (48). The identification with Napoleon reaches its climax in the vignette for chapter 64, where the illustration portrays Becky in exile, wearing a Napoleonic hat, with binoculars in hand, looking toward England.

As we know, however, Becky is never entirely defeated. She is half British also, and if she is noticeably a female Napoleon, she is also to some degree a female Wellington. She claims only to be "on the staff" (25) but is promoted by her admirers and victims. Rawdon tells her "By Jove, Beck, you're fit to be Commander-in-Chief" (16), and when the new Sir Pitt renovates his house in Great Gaunt Street, he makes her "general-in-chief over these arrangements" (44). In Brussels, under the shadow of literal warfare, the narrator pays her the ironic accolade of saying that: "No man in the British army which has marched away, not the great duke himself, could be more cool or collected in the presence of doubts and difficulties, than the indomitable little aide-de-camp's wife" (30). But, as this ambiguous French-British background suggests, her popularity and notoriety, her feminine but also militant and predatory behavior, her success and failure are all mixed, never absolute.

Such analogies between a fascinating, ambitious, and corrupt woman like Becky, and figures like Napoleon and Wellington, who also cynically manipulate their pawns and victims, prominently mirror the narrator's mock-heroic style and manifest his ironic stylistic purposes—especially as those purposes illuminate connections between the public and private worlds, between the prominent and the obscure, between the somber and the comic, between the grand and the ludicrous—but also as they illuminate the connections between literal warfare and the warfare within society at large. Except for showing us the genial relationships between Rawdon and his son, and between Dobbin and young George, the narrative depicts an appalling series of familial, not to mention other antagonisms, such as Sedley's coarse mockery of Jos and disdain for him, old Sir Pitt's hostility to Rawdon (expressed, for example, in terms of hyena envy [14]), Osborne's deranged anger at George, and the hatred of Steyne for his heir (47). Such relationships are the norm, not the exception in Vanity Fair.

If the warfare's murderousness is the ultimate betrayal of human brotherhood, and if Osborne and Sedley should be brothers but fail to be, so do those characters fail whose blood relationships might be expected to foster such closeness. Sir Pitt's first comment about his brother Bute is: "Looking after his tithes, [damn] 'un. . . . Will brandy and water never kill him? He's as tough as old whatdyecallum—old Methusalem" (8). The words of the narrator emphasize the military analogy (*battles, spoil*) and connect it to the motives of material greed and economic speculation: "These money transactions, these speculations in life and death—these silent battles for reversionary spoil—make brothers very loving towards each other in Vanity Fair" (11). The greed also of course makes brothers "loving" toward their sisters. Seeing through the hypocrisy of her family members, Miss Crawley wretchedly cries out, "They all want to kill me—all—all" (25), prompting the narrator's pitying but shattering comment: "The last scene of her dismal Vanity Fair comedy was fast approaching; the tawdry lamps were going out one by one; and the dark curtain was almost ready to descend." How extraordinarily he renders her life as a meaningless play!

Such corruption of human motives extends, of course, to the realm of international politics, as epitomized by the Congress of Vienna, convened after Napoleon was sent to Elba. Again the word *august* is used ironically to describe the greedy manipulators at the Congress, especially Russia, which wanted Poland, Prussia, which wanted Saxony, and Austria, which wanted Italian territory:

> The august jobbers assembled at Vienna, and carving out the kingdoms of Europe according to their wisdom, had such causes of quarrel among themselves as might have set the armies which had overcome Napoleon to fight against each other, but for the return of the object of unanimous hatred and fear. This monarch had an army in full force because he had jobbed to himself Poland, and was determined to keep it: another had robbed half Saxony, and was bent on maintaining his acquisition: Italy was the object of a third's solicitude. Each was protesting against the rapacity of the other. (28)

Being "jobbers" (which, in another context, is also a term for *stock-brokers*), they misuse public trust for partisan gain, attempting to steal a country and its people.

In response to the news of Napoleon escaping from Elba and landing at Cannes in March 1815 on his way to Paris to reassemble his army, the narrator imagines a panic at Vienna such as would "cause Russia to drop his cards, and take Prussia into a corner" (18), thereby establishing an analogy between international politics and a game of chance—an analogy that extends his earlier analogy between warfare and gambling: "war was raging all over Europe, and Empires were being staked" (12). Even an ironically personified Russia, however (represented at Vienna by Czar Alexander II), cannot be a victim in the important sense in which Amelia is, as a helpless individual human being. Behind her partially indifferent lover, who sees "no fun in winning a thing unless you play for it" (13), and who feels excited by the prospect of playing "the great game of war" (30), is another gambler, one who is utterly ignorant of and indifferent to the emotions of human beings like Amelia, as warfare in turn is indifferent to him and to all victims: "Yes; Napoleon is flinging his last stake, and poor little Emmy Sedley's happiness forms, somehow, part of it" (18). And if her happiness is bound up with the wars of that "august mute personage," so too is the significance of those wars mock heroically reduced by their effect upon a creature whose chief activities are "billing and cooing, or working muslin collars in Russell Square."

Perhaps the most devastating characterization of war, however, occurs as the narrator terms it the carrying out of "the Devil's code of honour" (32). False conceptions of individual "honor" provoke duels; false conceptions of national "honor" provoke mass slaughter. Warfare is Infernal because it brutally reverses Creation—especially the creation of human life. But the Infernal Gentleman does not provoke wars; humans do, and humans enthusiastically support it, just like the toadies at the Cuff-Dobbin battle. Accordingly, the narrator attributes warfare's foolish epic popularity to human hypocrisy and cowardice in one of his most stingingly satirical judgments: "Time out of mind strength and courage have been the themes of bards and romances; and from the story of Troy down to to-day, poetry has always chosen a soldier for a hero. I wonder is it because men are cowards in heart that they admire bravery so much, and place military valour so far beyond every other quality for reward and worship?" (30).

By contrast, this prose narrative offers a different perspective, not only upon warfare but upon hero worship. Amelia's innocence unfortunately permits her to see George as a hero. In fact, his shallow glitter constitutes much of his appeal, as the narrator's irony indicates: "She never had seen a man so beautiful or so clever: such a figure on horseback: such a dancer: such a hero in general" (12). This hero worship is much like Dobbin's at school, and it involves a similar self-debasement. Her later semicanonization of George is even more pathetic and reveals her need to develop a more adequate awareness of others and of herself. When George worships himself in the mirror, he sees a mere surface image that he naïvely inflates into that of an "Adonis" (5), but the observing Becky sees what she later characterizes to Amelia as "that selfish humbug, that low-bred cockney-dandy, that padded booby, who had neither wit, nor manners, nor heart" (67).

Hers is probably the most devastating exposure of a hero image in the novel, but the narrator offers an analogous image from more ordinary human life: that of the cowardly Belgian hussar and wooer of the Osbornes' maid, "her hero" (32). He bears the wonderfully ludicrous name of Regulus Van Cutsum, his first name coming from that of a Roman consul, but being undercut by what follows. Indeed, he enacts his name in life, going off to war with a full length of mustache, neatly attired, and "with pockets and holsters crammed full of good things" from the Osborne larder, but tottering back to Pauline, a "haggard hussar" with a dragging sabre that clinks up the stairs. He was "too good a soldier to disobey his Colonel's orders to run away." Whatever form hero worship takes, military or civilian, the inflation of Napoleon or of George IV, self-glorification or glorification by others, it is the recurring subject of the novel's mock-heroic satire. As the narrator of this novel without a hero rhetorically asks, "have we not all been misled about our heroes?" (62).

Any serious discussion of the style of *Vanity Fair* requires consideration of the narrative's brilliant individuation of speech. Perhaps by way of illustrating the fun of renewed recognition, and by way of seeking to evoke the characteristic and memorable voices of different characters in the narrative, and the ongoing, ever more complex interweaving of their accents, one might provide a representative catalogue of voices in the sequence in which a reader encounters them in the narrative:

"Have you completed all the necessary preparations incident to Miss Sedley's departure?" (1)

"Well, a booky as big almost as a haystack." (1)

"Mademoiselle, je viens vous faire mes adieux." (1)

"How could you do so, Rebecca?" (2)

"I'm no angel." (2) [to be compared with: "I am innocent" (53) and "I am innocent" (55)].

"It's evident the poor devil's in love with me." (4)

"I'm a liberal man; but I've proper pride, and know my own station." (6)

"You pretty little hussey. . . . " (8)

"What is money compared to our souls, Sir?" (10)

"What an abandoned wretch!" (11)

"I lay five to two Matilda drops in a year." (11)

"I adore all imprudent matches." (11)

"I adore her and that sort of thing." (13)

"The British Merchant's Son shan't want, Sir." (13)

"Who'd ha' thought it! what a sly little devil! what a little fox it waws!" (15)

"By Jove, Beck, you're fit to be Commander-in-Chief, or Archbishop of Canterbury, by Jove." (16)

"O stockbrokers—bankrupts—used to it, you know." (17)

"They all want me dead, and are hankering for my money." (25)

"Hould your tongue, Mick, you booby." (27)

"Sent me twenty pound, damned old screw. . . . " (29)

"I—I'm not a military man." (32)

"I must have a sheep-dog." (37)

"Who are you to give orders here? You have no money." (49)

"O how much gayer it would be to wear spangles and trowsers, and dance before a booth at a fair." (51)

"Am I right in my conjecture, that Mr. Osborne entertained a society of chosen spirits round his sumptuous board last night?" (56)

"I ask for no more than your love." (59)

Earlier we saw the ironically contrasting language of Miss Pinkerton—who, driven by her need to dominate, contrives to be linguistically "elegant" (1) by using a French-derived term, *bouquet*—and of her sister, who just blurts out the language of everyday (*bowpot*), and we understood how this antithesis establishes an enduring contrast in the narrative between people who need to inflate themselves linguistically (and otherwise), and people who are content with their inherited language. Among the former, we see another schoolmaster, Mr. Veal, who is avidly attracted to sumptuosity: "Am I right in my conjecture, that Mr. Osborne entertained a society of chosen spirits round his sumptuous board last night?" (56). Among the latter we see Old Sir Pitt, who enjoys remaining (perhaps wallowing) in his rural dialect—"farden" (7), "hussey" (8)—and intonation: "what a little fox it waws!" Our awareness of this linguistic aspiration or contentment, therefore, helps alert us from the start to motives of social climbing or lack of interest therein—which so differentiates the characters whom we meet.

Miss Pinkerton's speech clearly indicates her conception of language as a weapon in the battle to aspire socially; hence the comedy of Becky's trumping her with the use of French, and thereby winning their little game or battle—the first conflict of many in the narrative. Becky's successful use of French against Miss Pinkerton then helps prompt her subsequent rejection of the English language dictionary (with all of its dominating and often misused authority). Amelia is of course shocked at this act of insubordination, and her utterance, "How could you do so, Rebecca?," typifies her passive, reactive nature. Becky's confident reply, "I'm no angel" may be the utterance of a moment, but when, many years and chapters later, we hear the repeated claim "I am innocent," if we remember that earlier utterance and if we connect it with what we hear in chapters 53 and 55, we will be fulfilling one of our primary functions as readers: by bringing related passages together to discover the narrative's coherence, and, by active participation, to reveal its meaning—often, as here, ironic meaning.

When we hear characteristic utterances like these, we may well ask ourselves: How much do these people change? Rawdon's love for his son changes him, and Dobbin's belated rejection of Amelia helps to change him and perhaps her, but one sees few other changes of any magnitude. Most of the narrative's emphasis falls, rather, on how they and we are trapped within the images one constructs of oneself or that others construct of us and that we accept. One thinks, of course, of Jane Osborne as her father's victim, sitting alone in mirrored emptiness (42), or of Amelia as a victim of her own constructs, but also of the platitudinous Osbornes: George and his father. The emptiness of their pretentious language utterly reveals them and their entrapment. George's statement, "I'm a liberal man; but I've proper pride, and know my own station," is a perfect example of self-delusion because none of the three parts of that clichéd statement are true: he is a narrow-minded, self-inflated, social climber. The language is simply repeated from a stock of public phrases meant to conceal and thereby justify private hypocrisy.

His father's statement, "The British Merchant's Son shan't want, Sir," in spite of its pretended pride in social station, reflects his actual belief that being a merchant is not socially adequate, that mercantile earnings justify the younger generation's social climbing—indeed, almost demand it as a national duty—and that the possession of money justifies social respect (the epitome of snobbery, which Thackeray defined in *The Book of Snobs* as the petty admiration of petty things). Old Osborne's language reveals his aggressive materialism and his naïve notion that one can buy respect—a respect that, as we know, his son never receives, not only because he is transparently foolish, but also because he is a stockbroker's son, whose social aspirations only identify him as a potential victim to his impecunious, predatory social superiors. He is a joke, but through him we see not only the absurdity and grossness of such pretentions, but also the harshness of a stratified society, members of whose upper echelons often lack money, but disdain those who earn it and disdain their children as well.

One's attitude toward money, therefore, crucially defines one's attitude and behavior toward other human beings. Arrogantly revelling in the power that his money gives him over others, Steyne contemptuously dismisses his daughter-in-law with the brutally frank words: "Who are you to give orders here? You have no money" (49). Lacking the ability to form any close human relationship, Miss

Crawley finds herself alone with her money—unprotected, one might almost say, and therefore finally a desperately unhappy woman living amidst sheer, dehumanizing greed against which she can only cry out in lonely protest—pathetically and yet perceptively knowing that only her death will release the money so avidly sought by her relatives. Her brother Bute, being a mindless gambler who once *gave* odds of 100-to-1, thinks inevitably in terms of wagering, as he announces his preparedness to bet 5-to-2 that his sister "drops" within a year: his language reveals that he has no more feeling toward her than toward an animal dropping dead in a field. His nephew Pitt, feeling himself left out of Miss Crawley's will in favor of Rawdon and Bute, takes consoling refuge in religion, playing the role of an independent preacher until the prospect of inheriting her money after all makes him orthodox and no longer requires the hypocritical pretense that he sees money as an obstacle to the welfare of his soul. In his use of religion to mask his greed, he ranks as one of the narrative's most notable hypocrites—along with his aunt, Mrs. Bute, whose comment that Becky is "an abandoned wretch" reveals that she too has abandoned everything except schemes for money.

Rawdon temporarily professes gratitude toward "the old girl" (25) for her past benefactions, but when she subsequently gives him only £20, he calls her a "damned old screw" (29). Thankfulness, like money, is indeed transient in Vanity Fair. The slang also typifies Rawdon's speech because he has lived among a careless sporting, gambling crowd and because his lack of intellect prompts his thoughtless acceptance of the language of this crowd. To him, therefore, an attractive young woman is a "filly" (11), money is "tin" (14), a watch is a "ticker" (30), and pawning an object is putting it "up the spout." Because his money comes from his aunt, not his father, he speaks contemptuously of his father as "an old *put*" (a bumpkin) (11). Being captivated by Becky, "his dull soul" (16) sees her as fit to be not only Commander-in-Chief, "by Jove," but—with laughable incongruity—Archbishop of Canterbury, "by Jove."

Love, therefore, whether imagined or genuine, also creates roles for ourselves and for others. Imagining himself to be an irresistible Adonis, George thinks his role is not to love but *to be loved,* thereby emulating the behavior of Jos, of all people, who also thinks women exist to be victims of *his* charms (4). George's statement about Amelia, "I adore her and that sort of thing," therefore, clearly reveals its emptiness because the indifferent carelessness of the concluding words contradicts the opening phrase, thereby showing it to be a mere cliché. "Silly romantic" (10) Miss Crawley is also a purveyor of such clichés, as when she misleads Becky with utterances like: "I adore all imprudent matches" (11). Becky partly wants to be misled, however, because Miss Crawley also provides clear evidence that the images she projects of herself and of others are self-indulgent fantasies. Self-love and self-flattery prompt the role-playing of all these people, who give up their fantasies only with anguished reluctance—like Jos, when his terrified need to flee Brussels forces him to admit: "I—I'm not a military man" (32).

Dobbin seems to lack these self-centered obsessions, but he too, of course, has the unworthy motivations of someone living in Vanity Fair. His willingness to say, "I ask for no more than your love" (59)—however different this language and tone are from those of the other men—nevertheless reveals the acceptance of a debasing role created for him by another person: Amelia, who enjoys being the recipient of his commitment, but is unwilling to make a reciprocal commitment of her own. How refreshingly different it is to hear the comical affectionateness of a voice like Mrs. O'Dowd's: "Hould your tongue, Mick, you booby" (27). Although she dominates their public conversation, she respects his professional authority, refusing, for example, to leave Brussels "till I get the word from Mick" (32). She fondly calls him "my Mick" (27), and conveys a remarkably different attitude toward her spouse with the words, "Mick, . . . whatever ye du, keep yourself sober for me party this evening," than does Mrs. Bute telling her husband, "Mr. Crawley, you are intoxicated as usual" (11).

Mrs. O'Dowd seems to play her domineering Irish role without even knowing that it is a role—thereby prompting the narrator to refer to "the honest lady's eccentricities" (28). Consequently, we can see her as a complete contrast to Becky, who is, of course, the narrative's greatest and most knowing role-player. Because Becky calculates every gesture and action that she makes, and every speech that she delivers, even her boredom with her "success" prompts her only to conceive of a new role, as she tells Steyne, "O how much gayer it would be to wear spangles and trowsers, and dance before a booth at a fair" (51). What she fails to recognize is that she has just provided a metaphorical epitome of her entire life in Vanity Fair. Only Becky could have uttered that statement, and only Becky could have said, "I must have a sheep-dog" (37). Anyone else would have said "female companion," and have had the conversation continue in a literal way. By using the metaphor (knowingly, this time), she prompts a lively outburst from young Lord Southdown, who doesn't understand her, and then a whole series of conversational jokes about sheep, wolves, shepherds, the shearing of a Southdown, and the Order of the Golden Fleece. The passage not only introduces the sinister Lord Steyne, but also, in showing Becky's wit, reveals how she becomes a source of wit in others and how she succeeds in captivating them.

Such a remarkable individuation of voices extends, of course, to the narrative voice, which stands out in English fictional narrative—among other qualities, for what has been called its sympathetic mockery. Going through his various metamorphoses, however, he ranges beyond that central tone, extending from one of sharp satire, where the sympathy momentarily disappears, to one of pathos, where the mockery briefly drops away. So too his observing commentary can range from a brief phrase, often aphoristic, to extended discussion, and from remarks about revealing details of everyday life to those that draw upon the epitomizing archetypes of classical mythology or of biblical narrative. Above all, it helps to remind us that we are participating in a "Comic History" (50).

The lightheartedness of his comic tone appears, for example, as he characterizes excessive curiosity in telling us how Mrs. Firkin and Miss Briggs witness "accidentally, through the key-hole" (15) the scene in which Old Sir Pitt goes down on his knees and proposes to Becky. More usually, however, he uses the specific details of a scene or of a narrative passage in order to offer a generalizing observation or an illustration. Thus, when Becky attempts to please not only Jos but his mother by paying a compliment about his handsome appearance, the narrator observes that all mothers are pleased by such compliments to their sons, and then offers an extravagantly comical example: "If you had told Sicorax that her son Caliban was as handsome as Apollo, she would have been pleased, witch as she was" (3). In short, he indicates that one can hardly manage to flatter people too much. As he remarks elsewhere: "Who was the blundering idiot who said that 'fine words butter no parsnips?' Half the parsnips of society are served and rendered palatable with no other sauce" (19). In challenging the wisdom of a well-known aphorism, he offers one of his own.

In satirizing the prevailing conventionalism of universities, he pithily remarks that Pitt somehow failed to receive any prizes "in spite of a mediocrity which ought to have insured any man a success" (9). Pitt's later stinginess prompts a genuine aphorism: "To part with money is a sacrifice beyond almost all men endowed with a sense of order" (44). Here the sting is in the tail: the aphorism might have ended after "men," but then it would have lacked the brilliantly ironic final phrase, which pointedly identifies the hypocrisy with which humans conceal their avarice under the guise of a pretended virtue— "a sense of order"—not a vice, which it actually is. In commenting upon Mrs. Bute's vicious characterization of Rawdon, the narrator again makes a succinct generalization: "Yes, if a man's character is to be abused, say what you will, there's nobody like a relation to do the business" (19). Here he encourages our sense of recognition by using the word *Yes*, but he also feels that he may meet some sentimental objection from other readers, and so he tries to meet that resistance by anticipating it with a direct address ("say what you will").

At other times he momentarily takes responsibility for the generalization entirely upon himself, although he soon implicates the reader as well. After explaining how Becky avoids thinking about the destructive effects of her behavior, especially upon others, he remarks: "for my part I believe that remorse is the least active of all a man's moral senses—the very easiest to be deadened when wakened: and in some never wakened at all. We grieve at being found out, and at the idea of shame or punishment; but the mere sense of wrong makes very few people unhappy in Vanity Fair" (41). Here the rhythm of his sentences seems especially revealing. The opening generalization ("remorse . . . senses") leads to two phrases that develop the thought in complementary ways ("deadened when wakened," "never wakened at all"). This generalization then leads to a new one ("We grieve at being found out"), which is extended by a phrase that completes it ("and . . . punishment"), but this two-part qualifying statement then leads to a counterstatement ("but . . . Vanity Fair") that conclusively reinforces the opening generalization about remorse.

The narrator characteristically derives his human awareness from reflections upon mere everyday phenomena like letters. Beginning with a typical aphorism, he then enlarges upon its implications with a series of challenging injunctions to the reader, and finally offers some ironic "remedies":

> Perhaps in Vanity Fair there are no better satires than letters. Take a bundle of your dear friend's of ten years back—your dear friend whom you hate now. Look at a file of your sister's: how you clung to each other till you quarreled about the twenty pound legacy! Get down the round-hand scrawls of your son who has half broken your heart with selfish undutifulness since; or a parcel of your own, breathing endless ardour and love eternal, which were sent back by your mistress when she married the Nabob— your mistress for whom you now care no more than for Queen Elizabeth. Vows, love, promises, confidences, gratitude, how queerly they read after a while! There ought to be a law in Vanity Fair ordering the destruction of every written document (except receipted tradesmen's bills) after a certain brief and proper interval. Those quacks and misanthropes who advertise indelible Japan ink should be made to perish along with their wicked discoveries. The best ink for Vanity Fair use would be one that faded utterly in a couple of days, and left the paper clean and blank, so that you might write on it to somebody else. (19)

The human relationships that he evokes extend the initial generalization to include friend, sister, son, and lover, and also the emotions and gestures attendant upon such relationships. Comically drawing upon the everyday phrase, "There ought to be a law . . . ," he ironically implies that the only human communications that seem to have any lasting value are receipted tradesmen's bills; the latter appear to be the surest bulwark against time. Everyday advertisements prompt further reflections upon human life: in this case the advertisements of "quacks and misanthropes" who claim to have invented indelible black ink—quacks because nothing material survives time, and misanthropes because letters written in unfading ink would be a constant, indeed universal, embarrassment and source of pain. Here too there is a further sting in the tail because the "remedy" of having paper from which the ink faded in a few days would only illustrate our irrepressible family likeness to the people in his examples: we *would* write on it to somebody else the same fundamental nonsense—as time *would* reveal.

The narrative voice also from time to time pointedly expresses itself in the form of rhetorical questions. At times they draw upon typical human experience, as when Miss Crawley's treatment of the pecuniarily subservient Miss Briggs prompts his appeal to our experience: "Who has not seen how women bully women? What tortures have men to endure, comparable to those daily-repeated shafts of scorn and cruelty with which poor women are riddled by the tyrants of their sex?" (33). Similarly, we see how Maria Bullock's condescension toward Jane Osborne, as expressed in the statement, "I regard her as a sister, of course" (42), causes the narrator to ask: "what does it mean when a lady says that she regards Jane as a sister?"—a question whose amusing difficulty is compounded by the fact that Jane *is* the "lady's" sister, nominally, at least.

We can also see something of the tonal variety of these questions as the narrator reflects upon Old Osborne's mingled affection and selfishness regarding George, responding first with the quiet interrogation, "Which of us is there can tell how much vanity lurks in our warmest regard for others, and how selfish our love is?" (35), and then, after an exposition of Old Osborne's arrogant self-assurance, responding with the tartly summarizing and satirical question: "Always to be right, always to trample forward, and never to doubt, are not these the great qualities with which dullness takes the lead in the world?" The most devastating question (and implied answer) of all, perhaps, joins quietness and satire in epitomizing our entire isolation: "Who is ever missed in Vanity Fair?" (61).

These somber awarenesses inevitably produce the melancholy expression on the jester's face, but what reader can forget the exuberance of his comic mode? This wonderful narrative exhibits such a rich abundance of comic aspects that one could cite them endlessly. We see this exuberance, for example, in dozens of his names, from Glauber (11), who has to be a doctor (Glauber's salts); Cannon (12), who has to be a billiard player; Martingale (17), who has to be a gambler; Cinqbars (17), who has to be a sporting man; Pestler (38), who is inevitably an apothecary; and Hammerdown (17), who of course is an auctioneer (we need not even mention again names like Crawley or Steyne [stain]); to such names as we find in the array of clergymen whom Lady Southdown receives: "the Reverend Saunders McNitre the Scotch divine [clearly a fire-and-brimstone preacher]; or the Reverend Luke Waters the mild Wesleyan; or the Reverend Giles Jowls the illuminated Cobbler who dubbed himself Reverend as Napoleon crowned himself Emperor [the ultimate self-made man]" (33). Chapter 33 is in fact a little treasure house of satirical language, that not only identifies the clergymen, but also quack medicine, both physical and spiritual: "Podger's Pills, Rodger's Pills, Pokey's Elixir," and those wonderful tracts, "The Washerwoman of Finchley Common," "A Voice from the Flames," "A Trumpet-warning to Jericho," and best of all, perhaps, "The Fleshpots Broken; or, the Converted Cannibal."

These names epitomize human activities and attitudes, as do names like Dives (17, 57) and Lazarus (57) and Epicurus (17), but the latter names have greater generalizing power because they have been established in biblical writing and history. In a similar mode, the narrator gives an extended humorous summary of Rawdon's infatuation with Becky, and then caps it with mock-heroic analogies that comically reveal archetypal aspects of ordinary experience, and that join the realms of mythology and everyday life: "Is his case a rare one? and don't we see every day in the world many an honest Hercules at the apron-strings of Omphale, and great whiskered Samsons prostrate in Delilah's lap?" (16). "Were not Achilles and Ajax both in love with their servant maids? . . . If people only made prudent marriages, what a stop to population there would be!"

The Arabian Nights' Entertainments offers another archetypal expression of human experience in its metaphor for unrealistic expectations as articulated in the figure of Alnaschar. Early in the novel, at least, the narrator's irony is playful, as he evokes Becky's daydreams of her future life in India, and then comments: "Charming Alnaschar visions! it is the happy privilege of youth to construct you, and many a fanciful young creature besides Rebecca Sharp has indulged in these delightful day-dreams ere now!" (3). Later, in the vignette initial for chapter 52, however, we see a drawing of Alnaschar that ironically qualifies the manipulations of Lord Steyne, as he "Shows Himself in a Most Amiable Light."

Fiction joins history, or at least what passes for history, when Jos drinks the bowl of rack punch at Vauxhall, for the narrator immediately claims to see its parallel in the traditional accounts of the deaths of Fair Rosamond and Alexander: "Was not a bowl of Prussic acid the cause of fair Rosamond's retiring from the world? Was not a bowl of wine the cause of the demise of Alexander the Great, or at least does not Dr. Lempriere say so?" (6). Queen Elizabeth enters the narrative in order to accept good beer from "the Crawley of the day (a handsome gentleman with a trim beard and a good leg)" (7) and to reward him with a borough entitled to send two members to Parliament—or so "It is related." Understandably, the narrator feels unsure about the identity of "The Muse, whoever she be, who presides over this Comic History" (50), because this narrative, articulating as it does such a capacious range of human experience, and drawing upon such varied and yet complementary sources of inspiration, marks her first appearance—whoever she be.

Thackeray's narratives do not *conclude;* instead, they reach a moment of stasis. His endings are not endings, but pauses in an implicitly ongoing process. They therefore contain within them the potential for continuing, and indeed characters from one narrative may reappear in a subsequent one. These new beginnings are not really beginnings, however, any more than the endings were endings; rather, they are *reenactments.* That is the ultimate meaning of the puppet metaphor.

Obviously, therefore, a critic cannot arrive at the finality of conclusive remarks: one simply and reluctantly stops, recognizing that the conditions established by Thackeray's narrative require necessary, arbitrary limits. In this sense, serialization is a metaphor for the kind of narrative writing epitomized by *Vanity Fair*. The serial narrative suited Thackeray's genius because, among other reasons, it emulated one of his most basic perceptions of life "under the sun": endless reenactments amid the flow of time.

And like time, the narrative is unable to reach conclusion, to achieve the definitive, convulsive ending of Revelation. *Vanity Fair* does not yield to Revelation. Therefore, the pessimism of the Preacher of Ecclesiastes cannot be transcended: "The thing that hath been, it is that which shall be; and that which is done is that which shall be done: and there is no new thing under the sun." Logically, therefore, the narrative ends with abrupt arbitrariness: "Ah! *Vanitas Vanitatum!* Which of us is happy in this world? Which of us has his desire? or, having it, is satisfied?—Come children, let us shut up the box and the puppets, for our play is played out" (67). But the box that we see in the final illustration is *open,* because the puppet show will inevitably be many times reenacted. *That* awareness is the basis of subsolar comedy.

Notes and References

1.   Gordon S. Haight, ed., *The George Eliot Letters,* 7 vols. (New Haven: Yale University Press, 1954–56), 2: 349.

2.   Gordon N. Ray, ed., *The Letters and Private Papers of William Makepeace Thackeray,* 4 vols. (Cambridge, Mass.: Harvard University Press, 1945–46), 2: 772; hereafter cited as *Letters.*

3.   *The Sun,* 10 June 1847. Excerpted in Dudley Flamm, *Thackeray's Critics. An Annotated Bibliography of British and American Criticism 1836–1901* (Chapel Hill: University of North Carolina Press, 1967), 52; hereafter cited as Flamm.

4.   Henry F. Chorley, *The Athenaeum* (24 July 1847); excerpted in Flamm, 52.

5.   *Letters,* 2: 309.

6.   George Henry Lewes, *The Morning Chronicle,* 6 March 1848; reprinted in Geoffrey Tillotson and Donald Hawes, eds., *Thackeray: The Critical Heritage* (New York: Barnes and Noble, 1968), 46; hereafter cited as *Heritage.*

7.   *Letters,* 2: 354.

8.   Elizabeth Rigby, *The Quarterly Review,* 84 (December 1848); reprinted in *Heritage,* 80.

9.   Robert Bell, *Fraser's Magazine,* 38 (September 1848); reprinted in *Heritage,* 65.

10.   *Letters,* 2: 423–24.

11.   *The Sun,* 10 June 1847; excerpted in Flamm, 52.

12.   Lewes, *The Morning Chronicle,* 6 March 1848; reprinted in *Heritage,* 46.

13.   Bell, *Fraser's Magazine,* 38 (September 1848); reprinted in *Heritage,* 65.

14.   John Forster, *The Examiner,* 22 July 1848; reprinted in *Heritage,* 57.

15. Rigby, *The Quarterly Review*, 84 (December 1848); reprinted in *Heritage*, 79.

16. Samuel Phillips, *The Times*, 22 December 1852; reprinted in *Heritage*, 154.

17. Robert Rintoul, *The Spectator*, 22 July 1848; reprinted in *Heritage*, 58.

18. Letter from Charlotte Brontë to W. S. Williams, 29 March 1848; excerpted in *Heritage*, 51.

19. Bell, *Fraser's Magazine*, 38 (September 1848); reprinted in *Heritage*, 66.

20. Rigby, *The Quarterly Review*, 84 (December 1848); reprinted in *Heritage*, 79.

21. Phillips, *The Times*, 22 December 1852; reprinted in *Heritage*, 151.

22. Lewes, *The Morning Chronicle*, 6 March 1848; reprinted in *Heritage*, 44–45.

23. Lewes, *The Morning Chronicle*, 6 March 1848; reprinted in *Heritage*, 45.

24. Abraham Hayward, *The Edinburgh Review*, 88 (January 1848); reprinted in *Heritage*, 37.

25. Rintoul, *The Spectator*, 22 July 1848; reprinted in *Heritage*, 61.

26. Forster, *The Examiner*, 22 July 1848; reprinted in *Heritage*, 58.

27. Peter L. Shillingsburg, *Pegasus in Harness. Victorian Publishing and W. M. Thackeray* (Charlottesville and London: University of Virginia Press, 1992), 266.

28. *Letters*, 2: 318.

29. Whitwell Elwin, *The Quarterly Review*, 97 (September 1855); reprinted in *Heritage*, 237.

30. Lubbock, *The Craft of Fiction* (London: Jonathan Cape, 1921; rpt. New York: The Viking Press, 1957), 94–95.

31. Lubbock, 96–97.

32. Gordon N. Ray, *Thackeray: The Uses of Adversity* (New York: McGraw-Hill, 1955), 388.

Selected Bibliography

Primary Sources

Vanity Fair was published in nineteen monthly serial installments (the last one a double number) from January 1847 through July 1848 with illustrations by Thackeray, and then immediately republished in a one-volume edition.

The standard edition of the novel is that edited by Peter L. Shillingsburg (New York and London: Garland Publishing, 1989).

The standard edition of the correspondence is Gordon N. Ray, ed., *The Letters and Private Papers of William Makepeace Thackeray*, 4 vols. (Cambridge, Mass.: Harvard University Press, 1945–46). Edgar F. Harden has edited two supplementary volumes (New York and London: Garland Publishing, 1994).

Secondary Sources

Biographies

Monsarrat, Ann. *An Uneasy Victorian*. New York: Dodd, Mead, 1980.
Peters, Catherine. *Thackeray's Universe*. London: Faber and Faber, 1987.

Selected Bibliography

Ray, Gordon N. *Thackeray: The Uses of Adversity*. New York: McGraw-Hill, 1955.
──. *Thackeray: The Age of Wisdom*. New York: McGraw-Hill, 1958.

Criticism: Books

Colby, Robert A. *Thackeray's Canvass of Humanity*. Columbus: Ohio State University Press, 1979.

Flamm, Dudley. *Thackeray's Critics. An Annotated Bibliography of British and American Criticism 1836–1901*. Chapel Hill: University of North Carolina Press, 1967.

Goldfarb, Sheldon. *William Makepeace Thackeray. An Annotated Bibliography 1976–1987*. New York: Garland Publishing, 1989.

Harden, Edgar F. *The Emergence of Thackeray's Serial Fiction*. Athens: University of Georgia Press, 1979.

Hardy, Barbara. *The Exposure of Luxury: Radical Themes in Thackeray*. Pittsburgh: University of Pittsburgh Press, 1972.

Loofbourow, John. *Thackeray and the Form of Fiction*. Princeton, N.J.: Princeton University Press, 1964.

McMaster, Juliet. *Thackeray: The Major Novels*. Toronto: University of Toronto Press, 1971.

Olmsted, John Charles. *Thackeray and His Twentieth-Century Critics. An Annotated Bibliography 1900–1975*. New York: Garland Publishing, 1977.

Rawlins, Jack P. *Thackeray's Novels: A Fiction that Is True*. Berkeley: University of California Press, 1974.

Sutherland, John A., *Thackeray at Work*. London: Athlone Press, 1974.

Tillotson, Geoffrey. *Thackeray the Novelist*. Cambridge: Cambridge University Press, 1954; rpt. London: Methuen, 1963.

────── and Donald Hawes, eds. *Thackeray: The Critical Heritage*. New York: Barnes and Noble, 1968.

Tillotson, Kathleen. *Novels of the Eighteen-Forties*. Oxford: Clarendon Press, 1954.

Wheatley, James H. *Patterns in Thackeray's Fiction*. Cambridge, Mass.: Massachusetts Institute of Technology Press, 1969.

Criticism: Articles

Blodgett, Harriet. "Necessary Presence: The Rhetoric of the Narrator in *Vanity Fair*." *Nineteenth-Century Fiction*, 22 (1967–68): 211–23.

Dyson, A. E. "*Vanity Fair*: An Irony Against Heroes." *Critical Quarterly*, 6

(1964): 11–31; rpt. in Dyson, *The Crazy Fabric: Essays in Irony.* London: Macmillan, 1965.

Harden, Edgar F. "The Discipline and Significance of Form in *Vanity Fair.*" *Publications of the Modern Language Association,* 82 (1967): 530–41; rpt. in Arthur Pollard, ed., *Thackeray. Vanity Fair. A Casebook.* London: Macmillan, 1978.

Lester, John A., Jr. "Thackeray's Narrative Technique." *Publications of the Modern Language Association,* 69 (1954): 392–409.

Priestley, F. E. L. "Introduction." W. M. Thackeray, *Vanity Fair.* New York: Odyssey Press, 1969, pp. viii–xlvi.

Sharp, Sister M. Corona. "Sympathetic Mockery: A Study of the Narrator's Character in *Vanity Fair.*" *English Literary History,* 29 (1962): 324–36.

Taube, Myron. "Contrast as a Principle of Structure in *Vanity Fair.*" *Nineteenth-Century Fiction,* 18 (1963–64): 119–35.

Index

Index

Ray, Gordon N., 14, 17, 121n32, 122
Regulus, 107
Rigby, Elizabeth, 11–13, 120n8, 121nn.15, 20
Rintoul, Robert, 12–13, 121n17, 25

St. Paul's Cathedral, 81
Semiramis, 95–96
Shakespeare, William, 15; *Cymbelline*, 55, 74; *Midsummer Night's Dream*, 55, 75; *Tempest*, 114
Sharp, Sister Corona, 16, 124
Shillingsburg, Peter L., 13, 17, 121n27
Sutherland, John A., 16, 123
Swift, Jonathan, 78

Taube, Myron, 16, 124
Thackeray, William Makepeace: birth of, 3; creativity of, 3; personas created by, 4; development as writer of fiction, 4; as "the Fielding of the nine-teenth century," 12; as realist and focus on everyday life, 4–5; as writer of essays and books on travel, 4

WORKS
Book of Snobs, 110
Catherine, 5
Henry Esmond, 6–7
Newcomes, 6–7
Pendennis, 6–7
Thurtell, John, 43
Tillotson, Geoffrey, 15–16, 120n6, 123
Tillotson, Kathleen, 15, 123
Trollope, Anthony, 15

Victoria I, 3

Waterloo, battle of, 3, 32–33, 58, 60, 70, 98–99, 101, 103
Waugh, Evelyn, 15
Wellington, Arthur Wellesley, Duke of, 96, 98–100, 104
Wheatley, James, 16, 123

The Author

Edgar F. Harden graduated from the Lawrenceville School and received the A.B. degree from Princeton University and the A.M. and Ph.D. degrees from Harvard University. He is professor of English at Simon Fraser University, and has published numerous articles on Thackeray. He is also the author of *The Emergence of Thackeray's Serial Fiction* (1979), and *Thackeray's "English Humourists" and "Four Georges"* (1985), and has edited the standard critical edition of Thackeray's *Henry Esmond* (1989), *Annotations for the Selected Works of William Makepeace Thackeray* (1990), and two volumes of *The Letters and Private Papers of William Makepeace Thackeray* (1994).